TRANSFORMER

AWAKENING FROM A
SPIRITUAL COMA

TRANSFORMER
AWAKENING FROM A SPIRITUAL COMA

A
NICK SHAKOOUR
AUTOBIOGRAPHY

TABLE OF CONTENTS

FIGHT

Why do we have to fight for everything? Our survival, self-worth, love, and respect—it *makes no sense.* Sometimes it can feel like we've been placed on planet Earth as a convenient punching bag—*what is up with that?* People waltz into our lives like angels of light, then think it's fun to pull the switch and wreck us for sport.

Well, I say it's time to fight back ... with strength and love. Fight to shed light on the evil that attempts to seep into our lives, even by those closest to us.

We may be dragged through experiences that make us forget our rightful place in this world, but our true essence, gifted by our Creator, will always remain intact to remind us of who we really are. It's time to fight...

Spiritual Warfare-Style!

TRANSFORMER

AWAKENING FROM A SPIRITUAL COMA

ONE

A WAR-TORN UPBRINGING

LOOK! UP IN THE SKY! Is it a bird!? Is it a plane!? No—it's a missile that's headed straight to your house! **BOOM-BAM!** Explosions **GALORE!** Major civil war outbreaks were the constant in our country of good ol' Lebanon (1984). Beirut, Lebanon, that is! Mom once called it "The Paris of The Middle East." I'd think, *"Really? 'The Paris of The Middle East?' What part? The buildings riddled with bullet holes or the huge pile of post-bombing debris?"* Paris must have been one frightening place to live—*"Wi! Wi!" (Oui! Oui!).*

Mom wasn't playing around: Lebanon was a lively, European-infused Middle Eastern oasis known as *the* vacation hot spot worldwide. Boasting a uniquely varied climate, the country welcomed you to ski on its frozen Alps and tan on its sunny beaches in the same season!

Once a thriving country, the constant outbreaks of war would bring Lebanon crashing to its knees as it hopelessly spiraled into a black pit of endless chaos. Its reputation as *the* "hot spot" would take on an entirely new and unfortunate meaning.

Welcome to our little broken town of Bourj Hammoud! It may have been ghetto, but it was endearing in a *street rat—Aladdin-type* of way. Let's all say it together... It sounds like this: "Burrrrj Hammoooooood." There you go, you got it!

The people were boisterous and unafraid to get *all up in yo business*. Heck, strangers invited you to their place for afternoon coffee as bombings ran rampant in the distance. Yet despite constant threats, we always kept sight of how to have fun!

Enter **LUNA** (amusement) **PARK**: a place I lovingly call *"Ghetto Disneyland."* Visiting Luna Park was an absolute blast, even if the rides smelled like leaking gas and made funny noises. **GRENDIZER** was my **FAVORITE** ride—a sentient robot who transformed into a spaceship and was attached to a merry-go-round. I'd watch his animated series every day and passionately exclaim along in Arabic his famous catchphrase, **"Grendizer ... Entalik!"** ("Grendizer ... Take off!"). Grendizer made me believe in transformation—in saving people!

SUPERHEROES ROCK!

Two of my other favorites were Mom and Dad! They infused me with love and care and deserve major brownie points for having raised a family under such dire, war-driven circumstances!

Meet Mom, **Verjen**—*Her Superpower: connecting, empathizing, and healing people by openly sharing her heart.* By the way, Mom was also one mean cook, whipping up the best hummus and tabbouleh in the world!

Then we have Dad, **George**—*His Superpower: aggressively maneuvering and combating with strength and love.* Dad was in the Lebanese Marines during the '70s, and the guy would have taken a bullet for his family any day!

HOLD ON!

Let's quickly rewind to the night when both my parents risked having to do just that (taking multiple bullets)... while Mom was bursting at the seams (pregnant) with yours truly!

AND ... PLAY!

SPLASH!

Mom's water broke in the middle of a war-torn night, and little Nico *(that's me)* was ready to enter the world! Mom and Dad were rushed to the hospital in a taxi as it swerved all over the freeway, rapidly dodging missiles, as roadsides and nearby buildings were blown to smithereens! After being held captive in labor for three days, Mom finally evicted me (thank God), and there I was out in the open, screaming my naked little head off!

Mom and Dad were "The Protectors!" They never skipped a beat on making sure I felt loved and cared for, even as my baby sister Janet came along! Janet was like the cutest puppy you'd ever seen, combined with the most beautiful porcelain doll ever created. It was fun having a younger sister to feel protective of and admittedly also a little jealous of. Janet was an absolute blast to play with—we'd use our imaginations to teleport to different worlds, cut loose, and get carried away; imagination quickly became the key to our connection. It helped us temporarily escape the constant feeling of impending doom that enveloped our entire country.

My imagination would wreak havoc

&

confuse the daylights out of those around me!

My first victims—Grandma ("Teta" in Arabic) and her reusable shopping bag! By the way, **Grandma Mary** (Dad's mom) was a SAVAGE that you did not want to mess with— *Her Superpower: tearing your mind to shreds with one thunderous blow of her insult-loaded tongue!* But, underneath that Godzilla-like demeanor lived a sweet woman who truly loved her grandchildren.

While at Grandma's watching TV, my eye caught a glimpse of a reusable Christmas shopping bag that displayed images of colorfully wrapped gift boxes. Staring on curiously, an imaginative trance took hold! Convinced that there were real toys hidden behind those printed images, I grabbed a pair of scissors and relentlessly went to town on that bag—the toys would surely fall out from *"the other side"* at any second!

Snip, snip, and snip, but... NO TOYS! The bag was ravaged! After shaking it aggressively multiple times, nothing fell out—***bummer!***

Grandma peeked out the kitchen door, caught me in the act, promptly marched over, and yelled, "What are you doing to the bag?!" After explaining my *alternate dimension* toy theory to her, she looked at me like I was nuts but opted to allow her loony toon of a grandson to keep cutting ... and soon enough, the only thing that appeared was the other side of the apartment hallway through what had become a *holy bag*. With my head hanging in shame, the scissors were handed over to Grandma.

Mom's turn to play victim to my imagination would shortly follow. She was hosting her friend for afternoon coffee and had me play in the foyer of our apartment's stairwell. After growing extremely bored, it was time to head back inside, but the door was locked! A gentle knock, but Mom didn't answer! *Why would she lock me outside?*

A few more gentle knocks, and still no answer! Ahh, but my imagination had a perfectly plausible explanation: *"Oh, Mom wants her friend to think she's cool, and I'll just end up cramping her style—got it!"* So the only logical thing left to do was walk to Grandma's by myself. I'd be back way before Mom was done entertaining her friend anyway, so ... *no harm, no foul.*

There I was ... five-year-old little Nico ... taking a stroll through the streets of Bourj Hammoud ... like a stud—*"This grown-up thing is easy! I could move out on my own tomorrow!"*

Knock, Knock, Knock!

Grandma promptly opened her front door to find me staring at her calmly. She sharply asked, "Where's your mom?" To which I bluntly replied, "She locked me out of the house to have coffee with her friend and didn't want me around."

GRANDMA—ANGRY!
GRANDMA... MAAAD!!!

Urg! Urg! Huff! Huff!
How could her daughter-in-law have
done this to HER grandson!?
Lock him out!? To have coffee with a friend!?
The NERVE!

Grandma aggressively yanked me inside, handed me a refreshment, and ordered me to sit down while she got on the phone to tell Mom off. *Oh oh*—chugging the glass of juice rapidly, it was time to leave, but Grandma had already snitched me out, and Mom was now on her way after having desperately searched the streets—screaming my name out at the top of her lungs!

Moments later, a very frazzled woman burst into Grandma's apartment! She looked like she had escaped from an insane asylum. It was Mom: CRAZED Mom! She scanned her surroundings, then—*locked in on her target: ME—guilty as charged!* Mom viciously lunged at me like the T-1000 from *The Terminator* movie! Jumping on the couch to take cover was futile—WHAM! SLAP! SLAP! SLAP! Mom served up some intensely excruciating butt spankings as we both screamed and cried, while Grandma just screamed ... at Mom ... for being a *bad* parent. Mom later clarified the misunderstanding with Grandma. In hindsight, I should have knocked harder—*my bad.*

Most adults were bewildered by my imagination, except for one ... **John.** "BUH-BAAH!" It was the only phrase he could speak as a 21-year-old with a severe case of Down syndrome and autism. This gentle soul lived with his mother in our apartment complex, and he was like Groot from *Guardians of the Galaxy—His Superpower: stopping people in their tracks with his powerful outbursts!*

Whether John was happy, sad, or mad, he'd yell, "Buh-Baah!" He'd "Buh-Baah" all over town and make everyone around him uncomfortable in the process. **FINALLY** ... *someone I could relate to!*

John was simple, innocent, accessible, and just a downright good person. His favorite pastime: playing with used cardboard boxes that his mother would bring home weekly. John would play with them in our stairwell for hours.

As the thought of, *"What's so special about some smelly cardboard?"* floated around in my mind—it dawned on me! The dude was using his *imagination!* So I jumped at the chance to go all in with John, and we instantly became the best of friends, building everything from boats to cars to spaceships together. Sometimes, taking the lead too aggressively with John would instigate a very disapproving "Buh-Baah!" from him, and I'd deserve it.

Handling a rambunctious kid like me was a handful for most people, but not for one particular person: **Grandpa** ("Papou" in Greek) **Nickolas** (another one of my heroes)—*His Superpower—100% faith in God.* Grandpa was a Greek Orthodox priest in Beirut and was considered a saint by many—**I LOVED HIM**—Grandpa was my absolute favorite! There was this profound (unspoken) connection between us—he baptized me as a baby, and priesthood was his calling, not a vocation. Grandpa would passionately travel on foot to people's homes with a basket of blessings in hand, expecting nothing in return. Everything he did, he did for the Lord. People were always in awe of that presence around Grandpa—that Spirit of God. His faith was strong, and on one eventful day, it would be tested ... as he stared down the barrel of a rifle!

Enter...
THE PLEADING WOMAN

She was a distant neighbor of Grandpa's who frantically rushed up to him in a panic after her teenage son was kidnapped by insurgents (children of Christian households were targeted for execution at the time). After calming her down, Grandpa fearlessly marched into the insurgent compound, where he was met with raised weapons. When he announced he was there to take the boy back to his family, the insurgents threatened to kill him on the spot! Grandpa confidently ordered, "You can only kill me if God gives you permission to." Talk about a hero! Grandpa proactively excused himself, marched right into the depths of the compound, grabbed the kid, and marched right out while the insurgents were left incapacitated, unable to pull their triggers; *they didn't dare take a single shot.* That night, the boy was brought home to his very thankful mother, and Grandpa's 100% faith in God was once again a sight to behold.

Faith can be an incredible Superpower.
Sometimes, it can be all you have.

Mom, Dad, Janet, and I were hanging out with Grandma at her place while Grandpa was tidying up at church, just a few blocks away. It was a calm evening when—**BOOM!!!** A shockingly epic explosion sent us all flying to the ground as the apartment rattled, followed by another sonic **BOOM!!!** We struggled to rebalance ourselves—Dad lunged toward my baby sister Janet, immediately grabbing her, as Mom yanked me off the floor! After snagging some pillows and blankets, Grandma frantically followed us to the front door when—TA! TA! TA! TA!—shots were fired!

We spilled out onto the apartment stairwell with adrenaline pumping; it was flooded with panicked neighbors rushing to make it to ground level when—**BOOM!**—everyone fell to the wayside!

We took to the streets where everything was set ablaze! Bourj Hammoud had become an unrecognizably deafening war zone! The night sky was filled with missiles torpedoing toward us like meteor showers; a *quick* tug from Mom, and I was reminded to keep running!

Thousands of grief-stricken people dispersed in all directions as Dad frantically led us to a building that was under construction next to Grandpa's church; it had an underground parking garage that we could seek shelter in! Construction was Dad's trade, and he knew exactly where to hide!

While desperately running for our lives, we could see the reflections of fiery explosions coming from behind! We ran past a local sandwich shop, and not a split second later, a missile flew right at it, blowing the entire place up! There was no time to gauge the next air strike! It was time to embrace *faith,* stop rubber-necking, and just—*RUN!!!*

TRACTION!

I desperately tried to keep up with my family as Mom tugged violently at my hand while Dad cradled and protected baby Janet, and Grandma kept up with their stride! The bombings intensified—*my legs were beat!* More gunfire, more deaths—*I started tripping over myself!* Another **BOOM!** Completely and utterly overwhelmed, I was nearly ready to collapse when—**GRENDIZER!** A voice suddenly rose from deep within me and heroically proclaimed his famous catchphrase, **"GRENDIZER ... TAKEOFF!"**

SUPERCHARGED NICO!

Supernatural strength: it engulfed my entire body, seemingly transforming my legs into motorcycle wheels, catapulting me forward at what can only be described as *"FULL THROTTLE SPEED!"*

Grandpa! He was still at church!

Dad pointed us toward the underground parking garage entrance, urgently handed Janet over to Mom, and quickly split off to get him! When Dad made it to church, he found Grandpa standing silently, praying amidst the bombings.

Grandpa would spend 30 minutes with God before reuniting with us, and there was no convincing him otherwise! He told Dad to *leave immediately!*

While quickly scurrying into a dark underground parking garage like frightened rodents, we desperately tried to catch our breaths when—**BOOM!** The ceiling of the parking structure shook, diverting everyone's attention up toward the surface. We all feared the worst while impatiently waiting for Dad's return. Eventually, he made it back to us, and a half hour later, Grandpa did too.

My legs turned to rubber and gave out as I collapsed onto the ground, lying next to Mom, while hundreds of downtrodden people somberly spread their blankets on the cold cement, preparing a place to sleep.

Then ... a ruby-red yo-yo caught my attention; a little girl was gently playing with it and didn't seem affected by the war: she released the yo-yo with grace and tugged it back up with ease. As I desperately fought to stay awake, the yo-yo's mesmerizing up-and-down motion gently forced me into a deep sleep. The yo-yo was *released and retrieved.* My eyes were getting heavy—*released and retrieved.* Everything was going dark—*released and retrieved.* My eyes shut.

THE WAR WAS OVER

As they stepped into the daylight, Mom and Dad carried us through a sea of deceased men, women, and children. Their corpses ... sprawled over the streets of Bourj Hammoud. Buildings were left in piles of rubble while Grandpa's church remained intact, along with his apartment ... and ours.

Loss: it would soon play a significant theme in our lives. Grandpa had suddenly collapsed in the middle of his church service and was rushed to the hospital, where he was practically unresponsive to every visitor. When Mom asked if he wanted to see me, Grandpa turned to her and gently nodded.

Mom led me to Grandpa's bedside, where I quietly stood on my tippy-toes, attempting to get a look at him as he lay motionless with his back turned to us. After Mom softly communicated my arrival, Grandpa suddenly *flipped* mid-air, levitating for a brief second ... before abruptly landing back onto the hospital bed to face us! He gazed at me, reached out, and touched me.

Shortly after, Grandpa passed away, leaving us all devastated, especially Grandma; she was crushed. One day, she received one too many calls of condolence and ended up forcibly slamming the handset onto the receiver repeatedly! Grandma suddenly broke down and cried in desperation, snapped, then ripped the entire phone unit off the wall and violently flung it to the ground! I stood there watching her, wishing Grandpa could come back.

Grandpa was to be buried in his priest's robe, but who would be the one to dress him? Mom loved Grandpa; she revered him and rose to the occasion. At the morgue, Mom pulled Grandpa out of the freezer drawer to find that his nose was still bleeding ... and his tears, still running ... after having been frozen for *three* days. Mom gently dressed him in his priest's robe.

The view from Grandma's balcony was surreal as hordes of people proudly paraded Grandpa's casket throughout the streets; it was the day of his funeral, and there must have been thousands of people there! As his casket peacefully passed by below, his presence could be sensed.

Inspiration struck!

Quickly grabbing a notepad and pencil from inside Grandma's apartment, I returned to the balcony and sketched everything from Grandpa's casket to the people parading it around. When the adults came back after the service, I handed Grandma my drawing: "Look, I drew Grandpa's funeral." Grandma stared at it somberly and nodded.

Loss came in waves; Mom would get word from the States that one of her sisters (Starlette) had passed away due to health complications. Most of Mom's family had immigrated to California by the mid-'80s.

As Mom sat me down at Grandma's, she revealed that we'd be visiting a place called **"AMERICA!"** My soul rejoiced: "America" had a certain ring to it! *But there was a catch:* Dad would stay behind because of Lebanon's no-travel policy for entire families (ensuring the return of the traveling family member(s)). Mom, Janet, and I would visit the United States for Aunt Starlette's funeral and return to Lebanon—that was the plan. However, something in me sensed otherwise: America ... wouldn't be a place we'd visit. It would be a place ... we'd call home.

TWO

THE NEW WORLD

The *Armenian Spice Girls!* That's who Mom and her seven sisters were! So let's do some math here for a second, shall we? Take eight spicy Armenian sisters, marry them off—they spit out two to five spicy kids ... who each spit out a few spicy kids of their own—and well ... that's a *lotta* family! We were like hillbillies when asked about our relation to one another, with our long-winded response of, "He's my cousin's cousin's cousin, and his second cousin's first cousin's third uncle's..." (ya get the point!).

AMERICA BABY!

Mom, three-year-old Janet, and my six-year-old self eagerly anticipated the sliding doors to open at San Francisco International Airport as excitement surged through us! Our adrenaline was in full swing when—SWISH! Like magic, the customs doors parted as loud cheers caught us off guard! We were practically tackled with overwhelming hugs and endless kisses from aunts, uncles, and my *cousin's cousin's cousin's...* (just kidding). They swarmed us with bouquets of balloons and wildly scented flowers as we were whisked off to stay at Aunt Arpine and Uncle George's house in Burligame, California! It was a charming city saturated with colorful trees—the town looked like a pastel painting, for God's sake!

After meeting about a million relatives during our short stay, it was time to head back to Lebanon; however, one of Mom's sisters, Aunt Sona, would beg to differ! She urged Mom to make America our permanent home as Mom pushed back at what seemed like an outlandish sentiment. Aunt Sona wouldn't have it; she was a strong-willed woman of culture who worked as a master rug weaver at a posh showroom in San Francisco.

"What on earth is a master rug weaver Nick?"

Well... I'm glad you asked! A master weaver can take a handmade rug (or tapestry) with holes, and re-weave the damaged area to match the rest of the rug's (or tapestry's) design. After the carpet (or tapestry) is woven to perfection, the newly stitched area is taken through an extensive aging process by being beaten with hammers and sharp tools, so that it flawlessly matches the rest of the rug's (or tapestry's) natural wear and tear. A zero-value carpet (you guessed it ... or tapestry) can be worth over a million dollars when fully restored!

*Mom just so happened to possess this very skill;
she learned the art of weaving at ten years
old after being pulled out of elementary school
by her mom & forced into labor due
to her father's passing.*

Aunt Sona's place of work boasted upscale contemporary *meets* French Victorian: tapestries hung from the walls—multiple spotlights showcased their ancient designs. The place looked like a straight-up museum!

As Mom effortlessly completed a sample repair on an area of a damaged rug, the owners of the showroom were floored—they desperately had to have her at whatever cost! But Mom wasn't having it! She didn't want to entertain the thought of staying, especially with Dad stuck in Lebanon. The owners were now tasked with convincing Mom (an *Armenian Spice Girl*) to stay in America *(good luck!)*. They came back with this offer: if Mom agreed to stay and work for them, they would have their hot-shot lawyer handle all the paperwork to rush our permanent residency application with all expenses paid! *But where would that leave Dad? The same offer would be extended to him!*

WE STAYED!

Dad wanted us to, even if it meant potentially sacrificing years before he could ever see us again. The offer was a Godsend due to the escalating dangers back home; that was enough to sway Mom into starting over in America! So, with Dad's heartfelt blessing and the belief that we would one day reunite, a massive leap of faith was taken as Mom, Aunt Sona, Janet, and I moved into a mini townhouse on Carmelita Avenue: one of four cozy units nestled right next to each other and surrounded by tart berry bushes and scented trees—it was our new start!

Aunt Sona was an amazing second mom to us, but my yearning for a father figure grew; with Dad, Grandpa, and Grendizer slowly becoming distant memories, who would fill in for them? Optimus Prime—*that's who!*

A show called *Transformers* immediately captivated me while channel surfing, and when Optimus Prime appeared on the screen, he instantly became my American Grendizer / temporary "Daddy!" Optimus Prime was grounded, noble, passionate, masculine, and kind—he was everything a little boy could ever want in a father figure—someone to emulate.

But let's not get it twisted...

Aunt Sona was just as awesome! After all, she was our "Mary Poppins"—*Her Superpower: being practically perfect in every way.* Aunt Sona looked after Janet and me on her days off and enriched our lives in numerous ways, including teaching us how to eat a soft-boiled egg from a fancy egg holder! *"Disgusting,"* was the first word that came to mind, but with her Armenian accent, Aunt Sona reassured, "Oh no... *Dis* is how *de* rich *peepel* eat." She sold us on the idea, and the repulsive soft-boiled egg went right down the hatch! I even sat upright pretending to be rich; not bad for a kid sleeping in a cold parking garage just a few months back!

We learned everything from old-school Armenian dance to the health benefits of walking, hiking, and self-care. And by the way, Aunt Sona also loved herself a good old-fashioned scary story! Gather around for...

Aunt Sona's Cautionary Tale of... The Drug Addicted Kids!

Aggressively floating her way over to Janet and me, Aunt Sona got RIGHT in our faces to bark a dire order—**"LOOK, I'm only going to tell you this once, so listen very carefully!"** She raised her index finger and warned, "If anyone ever offers you any drugs at school, **DON'T** take it!" Janet and I immediately snapped back! Aunt Sona went on a freakishly conspiratorial tirade: "First, they'll give it to you for free so you can get hooked!" We didn't want to be hooked on ANYTHING! Aunt Sona ramped up her intensity, adding, "Then, when you want more, they'll start charging you for it, and you'll have to steal money from your parents!"

Janet and I were beyond disgusted with ourselves for theoretically being hooked on drugs and for potentially stealing from our parents! *How could we do this to them!?* We desperately wanted Aunt Sona to stop the madness, but it was too late: she was already lost in her storytelling, screaming out, "AND YOU'LL KEEP USING AND USING AND USING UNTIL YOUR FAMILY IS DESTROYED, YOUR HOME IS WRECKED, AND YOU'RE BOTH DEAD! **DEAD!** AND **THAT'S...** WHERE IT WILL END FOR BOTH OF YOU!"

The silent treatment...

Aunt Sona didn't say a single word as she stared at us like we were guilty as charged. Meanwhile, *"someone"* was about to be guilty of wetting the living room carpet: "We'll never take anything from anyone!"—Janet desperately nodded in agreement. Aunt Sona squinted her investigative eyes ... sized us up ... then raised her chin as she proclaimed with pride, *"Abreees"* ("bravo" in Armenian). We didn't sleep well that night.

Mission... Accomplished

Aunt Sona's dire warning wrecked us. Janet and I loved our family; Mom worked so hard to make a life for us while learning how to speak English, and the last thing we wanted to do was drugs! Mom's schedule was *grueling:* she would walk me to school for about fifteen blocks (with Janet riding on top of her shoulders), drop me off, then walk another seven blocks to take the train to her rug restoration job in San Francisco (with Janet still in tow). Mom took life by the horns *(cowboy style)*, pouring every ounce of herself into building a solid foundation for us as she paved the way for that long-awaited day when Dad ... would finally arrive!

THREE

FAMILY FUN TIMES

Dad!!! It took a solid year to get him to the States, but he finally made it, running at us with big hugs and kisses—our family was once again whole! That meant we needed our own place because it was about to get all cramped with Aunt Sona being a newlywed—*this townhouse ain't big enough for the six of us, partner!* So it was settled: Aunt Sona and her hubby would stay in the townhouse on Carmelita ... and we'd move into our new apartment on Paloma Avenue: a tiny building nestled in an enchanting neighborhood, shrouded with fairytale-like trees.

Living on Paloma would be the foundational core of our most sacred years in Burlingame, California, representing a time of harvest & celebration: a new place with the promise of a new beginning.

PARTY TIME!

Whether it was birthdays or anniversaries, there always seemed to be a minimum of 20-50 relatives (like I said, *lots* of cousins). Our spirited celebrations always offered delicious food, drinks, and dance. Full disclosure, though ... Sometimes the drinking part would get out of hand between feuding relatives, *WWE* style! These frighteningly entertaining brawls would often be birthed out of one guy insulting the cooking of another guy's wife; while enjoying a baklava dessert, you'd see a watermelon being flung at the wall! Fun times with spirited relatives!

At Paloma, *family* also came in the form of *The Singhs,* our lively neighbors from the upper unit, spearheaded by **Kamani Singh**, the matriarch—*Her Superpower: bringing light to darkness with a joyfully humorous persona.* She was downright incredible: working as a correctional facility officer by day and being a phenomenal wife, mother of two, chef (making the best chicken curry ever), and entertainer by night (the woman knew how to *"saaang"* on her '80s karaoke machine). Kamani grew up around the rough crowd during her teens, which added character to her off-the-wall sense of humor! She effortlessly connected with kids—heck she was one herself! Kamani would make lunch, entertain us with karaoke performances, and follow it up with creative storytime! She would do comedic voices while improvising a reading of Cinderella—she'd make the stepmother gangsta: *"Girl, who you think you is? You ain't goin' to no ball. You bes get-yo behind in the kitchen and start cleanin'!"* We all cracked up to the point of tears: storytime was fun, wild, and unpredictable with Kamani! Janet and I would egg her on to do more, as she'd regretfully warn, "Okay, you guys, I gotta stop. You're going to get me in trouble with your mom!" Kamani had a beautifully innocent heart; Janet and I loved her, and we still do to this very day.

Fictional stories can be a blast, but sometimes, non-fictional ones can be just as exciting! For instance, the story of...

AUNT ANGEL THE KIDNAPPER!

Mom's #1 rule when Janet and I were home alone was, "DO NOT OPEN THE DOOR FOR ANYONE, NO MATTER WHO IT IS, EVEN IF THEY SAY THEY'RE A RELATIVE! THEY COULD BE A KIDNAPPER!"

And of course, à la Aunt Sona's, *"The kidnapper will disguise himself as a relative to trick you"* scare tactic, the directive was loud and clear!

After school, Dad would drop us off at home by 3:30 p.m., then head to his shuttle-driving job at the car rental company, and Mom would get home from work at around 6:30 p.m. Janet and I had the apartment to ourselves for three hours: making sandwiches, watching cartoons, doing homework, and grabbing cupcakes. It was fun because we felt like adults in charge and took that responsibility seriously. *VERY...* Seriously! Remember—**KIDNAPPERS!**

On one dark and rainy afternoon, while watching TV, there was a sudden knock at the door; Janet and I froze in paranoia; our relatives knew about Mom's *no-visit* policy when we were home by ourselves, so who could this have been? Janet and I gave each other one look and knew immediately—

A Kidnapper!

After all, it *was* raining, and the skies *were* gray! Quickly turning off the TV, I hushed Janet and waited for the knocking to stop, but it persisted! Cautiously tippy-toeing over to the cordless phone, it was time to dial 911, but we decided to hold off until some clarity could be had on this dire situation.

Janet and I gently placed our ears against the door ... nothing but silence. Then, a familiar voice made us jump—"Kids, it's your Aunt Angel. Are you both okay?"

It was blessed Aunt Angel—she lived several blocks away and had taken her 70-year-old self on a long-winded hike to check up on us during the storm. Aunt Angel was held to a sacred standard in our family—a Mother Teresa. She was thoughtful, had gravitas, and it would have been anyone's honor of a lifetime to have had her grace their home, BUT ... my nine-year-old self wasn't buying it—*"Aunt Angel,' my butt! That's exactly what a kidnapper would say!"*

Reaching for the metallic speakeasy door knocker, it was gently opened as my beady little eye cautiously peeked through. My imagination went into overdrive: *"WOW! The kidnapper looks just like Aunt Angel! Uncanny!"*

Right then, the *"imposter"* suddenly locked eyes with me!

I violently flung the speakeasy door shut, quickly hit the floor, landed right next to Janet, and whispered, "That kidnapper is dressed just like Aunt Angel!" Janet's eyes went wide!

Under the heavy downpour of rain, Aunt Angel's voice grew weary as she begged, "Please open the door, kids. Don't be scared. It's me, your Aunt Angel ... I'm soaking wet out here!" Janet and I darted frightened looks at each other, *knowing* it was a trap!

At that moment, I decided that fear had to go ... so that a higher purpose could be fulfilled... *PROTECTING MY LITTLE SISTER!* It was time to be brave ... *like a real superhero!* It was time ... *to confront this FREAK!*

Standing back up with full command, I aggressively reopened the speakeasy door, demanding, "How do we know it's you!?" Aunt Angel begged, "It *is* me. Please open the door ... it's cold out here!" The woman was catching pneumonia by the second, but my imagination had already taken its stronghold, and *"this MAN"* was not about to pull one over on us! The speakeasy door was *SLAMMED SHUT!*

Poor Aunt Angel had to fend for herself under the cold Bay Area rain for over an hour that evening. Mom made it home to find her drenched, sitting on our apartment staircase, resembling a beggar woman. We heard an earful from Mom that night as Aunt Angel sat there on our couch, shivering, while staring off into the abyss—*good thing we didn't open that door!*

FOUR

MY SUPERPOWER

CARTOONS! My passion for animation grew to astronomical proportions, with shows like *Transformers, Care Bears, Ninja Turtles, Inspector Gadget, and DuckTales!* The characters were awesome—they stood up to do the right thing and possessed moral standards that straight-up inspired me! Heck, Scrooge McDuck taught me the value of a dollar!

While watching these shows, I'd emulate the characters' voices and eventually, this obsession would crossover to real people: teachers, classmates, relatives, and strangers—all while being further encouraged and egged on by Mom to perform at every turn—especially at family gatherings; she had the same innate ability as a little girl and saw a lot of herself in me!

With family, I was the life of the party (Superman), but at school, I was the shy immigrant kid (Clark Kent) who kept his head down and did his work. My favorite subjects were Art, English, and Physical Ed (P.E.). Art allowed me to effortlessly draw and paint to my heart's content, while amazingly imaginative stories were read in English. Now, as far as *P.E.*—don't even get me started! It was flat-out *FUN, because* **RUDY BENTON** happened to the world! And thanks to him, my hidden ability to emulate people would be exposed at McKinley Elementary!

The Award for Best P.E. Teacher goes to ... **RUDY BENTON**—*His Superpower: nurturing and refueling YOUR Superpower.* The dude was the best P.E. teacher in the entire universe of P.E. teaching! Imagine having Doc Brown from *Back To The Future* as your instructor! Mr. Benton was EVERYONE'S favorite: the guy loved all his students and was super inspiring with how passionately bonkers he was about health, fitness, nutrition, and life itself! He encouraged dance as an essential part of exercise while playing songs from bands like the *B52s* and other hits from the '70s and '80s!

On one fateful day, Mr. Benton would unknowingly change the trajectory of my entire life forever.

At the start of each class, Mr. Benton would share health tips in the form of a mini monologue on the gymnasium stage. One day, he brought up the subject of the diaphragm and asked for volunteers to get up on stage and make the rest of the class laugh so that all of us could experience our diaphragms at work.

As each of my classmates got up on stage and did their goofy thing, a strong desire to perform overtook me! My pulse sped up, my breathing got heavier, and my palms were sweaty! The urge to do impressions was overwhelming, but did I want to put myself out there? Performing for family gatherings was fine ... but ... *for public display!?*

Mr. Benton gazed over his students and playfully asked, "Are there any final volunteers?" It was now or never: *my hand darted up with full force!* Mr. Benton took pause, and stared at me in confusion as some of the kids chuckled at the notion of *me* ... being in the same sentence as the word ... *funny.*

My heart was ready to burst out of my chest while standing on stage, as my genuinely confused classmates looked on—*what was I even thinking raising my hand!?*

Mr. Benton gave me the go-ahead, and after a few seconds of awkward silence, my nervousness suddenly transformed into what can only be described as *confident creativity!*

The auditorium vanished before my eyes—it was no longer me who was up on that stage ... it was "Mr. Geer," our history teacher! While emulating his snail-like walk, a drawn-out announcement was made in a deep voice; *"I'm a robot, and that's why they call me 'Mr. Gear,' because my GEARS move ... very ... very ... slooowww."*

Uncontrollable laughter erupted from the class as their electrifying reactions energized my next impression of ... the always intimidating ... Miss Castello: our hefty yard duty lady who sported a semi-spiked haircut and had an affinity for mono-chromatic jogging suits; she accessorized it all with a whistle lanyard around her neck and was a huge fan of hardcore gum chewing!

In a *manly* female voice, I shouted, *"SIT DOWN and finish your lunch!"* The class was dying of laughter while a comically-altered version of the *Mr. Potato Head* jingle was sung: *"It's Mrs. Castello Head (smacked my mouth to make a "POP" sound), and her bucket of parts ... buckets of fun for everyone!"* The students convulsed back and forth, flabbergasted and scream-crying with laughter!

Temporarily breaking free from my creative trance, I turned toward Mr. Benton, who was no longer in his chair; instead, he was on the floor in the fetal position, bear-hugging himself—exploding with agonizing laughter—his beet red face was about to burst! After noticing my bewildered stare, he gestured for me to keep going with the roll of his index finger. The show went on and on until— *RING!!!!!*

The students gave a standing ovation and were excused. Mr. Benton waddled over, placed an exhausted arm on my shoulder to stabilize himself, and *confessed,* "Kid, you are *really* funny!" He then asked, "Would you do this for all my classes today?" *Have fun for an entire day?! Ah...* **YEAH!**

While at the principal's office, Mr. Benton and I sought permission from the honorable Mr. Harron, who shot down the idea with a firm, **"ABSOLUTELY NOT."** Mr. Benton begged, "You *have* to see what this kid can do, he's *very* talented!"

That was the first time someone had defined this *thing* that was in me: TALENT.

After a spirited discussion, both educators reached a compromise: I could do my little improvisational show, BUT only once ... and it would have to be for the ENTIRE school!

A few hours later, while standing behind the heavy velvet curtains, anxiously awaiting my fate, the sound of the gymnasium filling up on the other side almost gave me diarrhea! All the teachers were out there, unsuspecting of the *roast-fest* headed their way!

Mr. Benton was off to stage left with rope eagerly in hand. After noticing my trepidation, he offered up, whispering, "You're going to be great! Just do what you did in my class!" He then drew the curtains with full gusto!

There I was ... nine-year-old little Nickolas ... facing the entire faculty and student body: all two thousand of them.

Desperately wanting to be funny, my mouth let out a crackly voice right out the gate—*yikes!* Trying to bounce back from the first disaster of an impression, I bombed instantly on the second try—*just shoot me!* Nothing but crickets—a single cough echoed in the gymnasium; the embarrassment was so real; my face heated up, and the desire to run off that stage took hold!

Then...
Something stopped me...

While gazing over a sea of students and faculty, a realization hit; there was nothing to be afraid of—nothing left to lose!

IT WAS ALL SYSTEMS GO!!!

Everyone instantaneously roared with laughter as a tidal wave of love splashed and crashed all over the gymnasium! My 1-hour improvised stand-up routine brought the entire house down, and even Miss Castello was cracking up: it turned out that underneath all that serious gum-chewing, she DID have a sense of humor after all—who knew!?

As I stood on that stage, immersed in my element, an unforeseeable ripple effect was set into motion. Mr. Benton had broken the shackles of shyness, by shining a massive spotlight on my *Superpower:* **Transformation**.

FIVE

THE "GREEN" CARD

Our long-awaited day as an immigrant family had arrived! Our green card application was approved, and my 11-year-old self was very excited about what was assumed to be a literal *"green"* (colored) card. My parents made it seem like it came with special privileges, so after asking Dad if it got us free meals at restaurants, his answer was, "No," and what a bummer that was! For a brief moment, I could picture myself holding the *"green"* card up to the waiter, insinuating, *"Yup, I'm covered."*

We had to leave the United States to get this *"green"* card and re-enter to make it official.

People usually flew to Canada and back for this process, but Mom and Dad had a different idea: we would fly back to Beirut, Lebanon, to visit Dad's side of the family.

While anxiously inquiring with Mom if it was safe to go back, she confidently waved me off, "Oh, it's fine... The bombings don't happen as much as they used to." Very reassuring!

The bombings may not have caused us any issues, but our flight sure did—the flight from *hell*, that is! On the way to Beirut, our brilliant pilot decided to *wing it* and fly right through a violent thunderstorm: our plane suddenly dropped without warning, swerved all over the place, and took a deep nosedive— rattling intensely! Lightning struck near the wings as people bounced in their seats! Janet and I screamed and cried in desperation as Mom steadied us from behind while Dad's whiskey intoxication offered up, "Just calm down; *it's going to be fine.*" Not a split second later, emergency signs lit up, signaling for an evacuation—at thirty-five thousand feet! This was it—we were going to die on some crappy airliner, all because we wanted some stupid *"green"* card that didn't even get you a free meal at a restaurant!

WE MADE IT TO BEIRUT!

But would we make it out alive? You see, good *ol'* Uncle Steve decided to take us all to Junieh Beach (a trendy beach in Beirut), where we would get stuck in an egg-shaped funicular! This part-metal, part-glass funicular was situated at the base of the beach, from where it lifted you into the air and glided across the freeway (while hanging from a thick cable) to the top of a mountain where a gigantic statue of Mother Mary (the Our Lady of Lebanon Shrine in Harissa) is nestled, right on top of a church. It was a major tourist attraction and a pilgrimage for many, but for us, it ended with experiencing the joy of Beirut's infamous rolling brownouts!

*Step right up ladies and gentlemen ... and ride the ride everyone's talkin' about! The amazing ... **Funicular!** That's right folks, it'll leave you hanging hundreds of feet above treetops for 45 minutes! You heard that right, **45 MINUTES!** Step raiiight up folks and experience certain death like NEVER BEFORE!*

THE FUNICULAR!

We found ourselves aggressively rocking side to side in mid-air as the gusty wind relentlessly challenged the strength of the cable that our funicular was attached to! The cars on the freeway looked like tiny ants! Mom, Janet, Cousin Nicole and I were in one funicular ... while Dad, Uncle Steve, his wife Rita, and their other daughter Stephanie were in another. It was so much *FUN!* We didn't care if the power ever came back and were perfectly happy, potentially plummeting to our deaths; after all, it was all in good fun— or should I say, *"FUN-icular!?"*

To our relief, the generator kicked in, and we made it back to ground level, where Janet and I had a good cry; we just wanted to go home, but at least the worst was over. We'd be visiting a friend of Dad's that evening for a relaxing dinner, and it's not like we were about to find ourselves trapped inside his tiny apartment elevator ... were we? Oh yes ... yes, we were! And why? Because the *FUN* ... had only just *BEGUN!*

THE TOWER OF TERROR

Being trapped in a malfunctioning, pitch-black elevator was nerve-wracking! After a prolonged awkward silence, Aunt Rita offered up some encouragement: "We're going to die!"— *inspiring words to live by.* It turned out that some access weight needed to be unburdened from the elevator, so all Dad and Uncle Steve had to do was jump up and down until it incrementally moved to the desired floor. *See? Easy peasy!* Janet and I had another good cry, knowing it wasn't our flight or the funicular that would do us in; it would be the *Elevator of Death* after all!

Luckily, our visit wasn't all scares: great times were had with family and friends throughout Christmas and the holidays—we stayed at Grandma Mary's. She was still her feisty old self and lived in the same apartment. Not seeing Grandpa there was surreal; he was missed and could still be sensed.

As Grandma Mary rushed in and out of the kitchen one day, arms loaded with glass bottles of soda and appetizers, she revealed, "I'm throwing you a birthday party."

Our return to the States was drawing near, and Grandma wanted to send me off with a big bang, so she called up as many relatives and friends as possible! She even ordered a fancy cake from the best spot in town!

After reminding her, "My birthday isn't until March," Grandma continued busying herself and revealed, "I won't be alive long enough to see your real birthday." *My heart broke in half.*

Enjoying Grandma's company was my primary focus that day, and if this was going to be my last hurrah with her, it would be cherished.

The birthday party was packed with cousins, aunts, uncles, and friends. Grandma bluntly threatened everyone to bring me high-quality gifts—or else! You have to appreciate Grandma: loving yet pushy and the prime example of someone appearing grumpy on the outside while being tender-hearted on the inside. That was the last time we all got to see Grandma. Shortly after our return to the United States, we would sadly hear of her passing.

I love you, Grandma.

SIX

BIG CHANGES

Mom was pregnant! Janet and I wondered, *"How could this have happened?"* Then, a realization of, *"Ohh... EW!"* shortly followed. It was time to get a bigger apartment, which meant leaving all of Paloma Avenue behind; the Singhs, walking down to Broadway Avenue for groceries, Nintendo game rentals—all of it.

What a bummer—we were about to move away from THE MOST FAMOUS STREET in the ENTIRE WORLD!

This Lost-In-Translation Moment...
Is Brought To You, By Nick & Janet.

Growing up as immigrant kids who were raised triracial and spoke multiple languages, experiencing lost-in-translation moments when it came to American pop culture, was par for the course. Janet and I would be left dumbfounded, every time we'd hear a character on a show or movie, express their ultimate dream: *"Making it ... on Broadway!"* Now admittedly, our beloved Broadway *was* a charming street, but nothing to write home about. Why were these characters obsessed with wanting their, *"...name up in lights,"* on Broadway? The only notable thing that ever happened on Broadway was our annual food festival, which featured a lively puppet show, but that was about it.

Janet and I would look at each other, shake our heads in disbelief, and giggle at the thought of anyone wanting to be, *"...SEEN on BROADWAY."* However, we felt very privileged. After all ... we lived right down the street from one of the world's most coveted destinations (insert facepalm).

Goodbye Paloma *(and "Broadway")*—hello Sanchez Avenue! It was a spacious two-bedroom / one-bath apartment on the second floor of a four-unit building. It even had a foyer right when you walked in—*a freaking foyer!* If anything is going to make you feel like you've made it as an immigrant family, it's a foyer right inside the entrance of your apartment!

Large windows blanketed the walls, displaying a front-row scenic view of bustling El Camino Real: one of the most famous streets in Burlingame (albeit not worldly renowned like "Broadway"). El Camino was lined with towering eucalyptus trees, which far outgrew the surrounding houses and apartments, creating an exotic dichotomy of jungle *meets* suburbia. It was the big daddy of all roads in our town, and its unique forest-like look made it hypnotizing to drive on.

Our new move was coupled with my continuation of Jr. High School at B.I.S. (Burlingame Intermediate School) ... or as I call it ... *hell.*

Gone were the days of childhood innocence for many of my classmates, and in came their obsessive need to become *adults:* they aggressively acted out, were relentlessly mean, and freely picked on others while making it a point to place targets on those who represented anything close to kindness and decency.

Slurs and hurtful words became the constant at school: the ridiculing and bullying wouldn't stop. Focusing in class became difficult while being picked on because of my ethnicity and looks—it crushed a lot of my self-confidence and self-worth, making me feel less than—like there was something wrong with me.

One day during science class, the kids at the table decided to comically make fun of my face as one of the girls condescendingly advised, "Seriously, why don't you just go get plastic surgery? You need it." Awkwardly laughing it off didn't help in warding off this witch. She persistently pushed back, "No, I'm being serious. I'm not joking. You're ugly; you should consider it."

As the other kids at the table piled on the insults, humiliation brought tears to my eyes, and my hand was raised. After asking the teacher if she could tell them to stop, these were her words of encouragement: "That girl's mother teaches at McKinley Elementary, and she would never say anything like that. She comes from a good family."

To survive junior high, energetically removing myself from my surroundings at school became a secondary *Superpower: Invisibility—like a turtle retreating into its shell.* Only within myself was some form of solace found, as most of lunch was spent on a deserted stone ledge—it was an hour of uninterrupted bliss! Eventually, a humorously chubby freckled kid named Peter (who was also made fun of) would join me. We were like two ships passing peacefully at sea.

Being picked on, straight up sucked ...
but the reclusiveness it inspired encouraged
me to explore my artistic passions on a much
deeper level: drawing capabilities advanced,
character voices multiplied, & passion
for videography took flight.

After finishing my lunch, I'd head to the library, ask for blank poster boards, and passionately sketch characters of various kinds—transmuting my deep hurt into a source of creative fuel (I had gallons worth). Drawing characters, while softly speaking in their voices, quickly turned into a stress reliever. Students passing by took notice, as others approached to see what all the fuss was about—a lively crowd eventually formed, borderline screaming out character sketch requests! A student would aggressively call out, "Hey, can you draw *(so and so),*" and to everyone's amazement, that character would be sketched within seconds as another student would simultaneously demand, "What does he sound like? Do his voice!"

Almost every day at lunch, these rowdy kids came by to check out my "sketch" show and, in doing so, were briefly reminded of something sacred they had left behind ... *their childhood innocence.*

Who cared about a social life at school anyway? It wasn't on my priority list; friends were nonexistent, so hanging out with family was the top priority. Family plus one, that is, with the birth of baby sister Mary! While holding her in my arms, the fragility of life was on full display with her tiny little face, cute little hands, and stubby little feet. Mom named her after Grandma Mary in honor of Dad's mom.

Capturing cute Mary moments with Dad's camcorder became an obsession, igniting a passion for filmmaking; Janet and some of our cousins would double as my on-camera actors. Inevitably, my love of storytelling and doing voices merged: Dad's camcorder was pointed directly at the TV, the volume was muted, *play* was hit on the VHS, the *rec* (record) button on the camcorder pressed, and every character in the animated film of my choosing, was voiced from beginning to end in one fell swoop!

Creative expansion took flight and eventually, my geeky buttoned-up self transformed into a laid-back, baggy-jean-wearing, *snarky* high schooler.

BURLINGAME HIGH SCHOOL!

It was everything you'd think high school would be. As a fun fact, Burlingame High made a cameo appearance in the opening sequence of the Michelle Pfeiffer movie *Dangerous Minds:* it was made to look run down and the name was changed to "Parkmont High School."

English, Art, and P.E. continued to take front and center as favorite subjects, but English was my ultimate favorite.

Mrs. McLaughlin—*Her Superpower: captivating your heart and mind.* The woman was part educator, part hippy, and part Mom away from Mom, always sharing with us her radiant smile; she genuinely cared about her students, and that was something you couldn't fake. Mrs. McLaughlin was all about intense discussions about life, politics, belief systems, and imagination! She was a Renaissance woman who exposed us to multiple works of Shakespeare and novels like *1984* and *Brave New World*. If Mrs. McLaughlin's English class were the only subject taught at Burlingame High, attending would be worth it!

CLIQUES

I mostly hung out with my cousin Sed and his fun-loving Armenian friends at first, then broke off to expand my horizons with various cliques. There was a whole buffet of humanity out there—options had to be explored. Wanting to experience high school from various vantage points fed my innate desire to relate to all kinds of *characters,* no matter how *different* they were from me.

SENIOR YEAR!

The jokester in me was in full swing—life was fun! Having fulfilled most of my units required for graduation, the school day would be over by noon! Drama was strategically selected as my final class ... to maximize the feeling of ending the school day even earlier! Pretty smart huh? Hey, it *was* drama class! *Hellooo... Kickback-Ville!*

Not so fast buddy...

Mr. Friberg was our larger-than-life acting teacher, and the guy towered above us: he was one intimidating dude who conducted his class with the utmost respect for the art *(so much for "Kickback-Ville")*. To show how serious he was about the craft, Mr. Friberg sprung a surprise assignment on us... We'd be performing, at minimum, a two-minute monologue on stage in front of the entire class! *Nooo!*

"Drama class was supposed to be a no-effort situation! Perform a memorized piece on stage? How was someone like me supposed to do that!?"

I stuck out like a sore thumb in a class of aspiring actors who obsessively bared their souls at every turn while I obsessively ensured that my slicked-back hair was held perfectly in place.

Luckily, a compadre in class was found—Ramy: an awkwardly joyous Egyptian (a bit chubby with a bowl-shaped haircut) who took the class for similar motives and whose hopes of smooth sailing through it were also crushed. We connected by poking fun at *actor culture* and thought that most of our classmates should be institutionalized.

MONOLOGUE WEEK

Mr. Friberg sat stoically in the front row of the theater, with pen and paper in hand—Ramy and I sat way in the back. The performances bored us to death! Leaning over to Ramy, I whispered smart-aleck responses every time an actor held a dramatic pause on stage (and there were PLENTY). Ramy chuckled uncontrollably and waved me off.

Mr. Friberg would try to periodically catch us in the act, and we'd immediately go deadpan!

Another student took a bow after finishing her agonizing monologue (listing off every man she'd ever *"dated,"* in the most nasalized voice). Her piece dragged on for what seemed like FOREVER, and it was TORTURE!

She walked off the stage to a smattering of applause—it was the final straw—these drawn-out monologues were KILLING me! I turned to Ramy (as the applause continued), opened my mouth, and with full-volume, sarcastically suggested (as the applause SUDDENLY stopped), "She could have just spared us the five minutes and said, *'Hey everyone, I'm a wh***.'*"

My voice echoed loudly inside a DEAD SILENT auditorium! Ramy gasped in shock and placed his hand over his mouth! Mr. Friberg didn't turn around this time. Instead, he ordered, "Nick... Come see me after class".

Sheepishly making my way over to Mr. Friberg, I crouched before him as he stood silently, staring daggers at me. He sized me up for a few uncomfortable seconds, then broke his silence and lectured, "Don't you know it's not nice to make fun of other students? Your classmates worked hard on their monologues, and I heard every remark you made back there." *Yikes—where was the nearest hole!?*

As his mental gears turned, Mr. Friberg's attitude shifted into an uncomfortably playful demeanor. After a short-lived pause, he made a statement that seemingly came out of left field—"You're a very talented artist." After noticing my confused reaction, he clarified, "I saw the picture of *The Beatles* (rock band) you drew on Courtney's binder," then, added, "I'm giving you after-school detention for the rest of the year."

I screamed, "What?! No!" Mr. Friberg pointedly explained, "You'll come in after school every day for an hour and paint the backdrops for our up-and-coming school play. We'll put that drawing talent of yours to good use."

Mr. Friberg didn't even care that I was off at noon; in response to my plea, he bluntly offered, "Well, now you can leave an hour later."

I wanted to claw his face off!

My senior year privilege was ripped away in an instant and that extra hour of freedom would be wasted, hanging out with a bunch of drama nerds—ugh!

Mr. Friberg sarcastically reminded me, "It's your turn next week... Have you been working on your monologue?" I hadn't even bothered but reassured, "Oh yeah, yeah, uh huh." Mr. Friberg smiled, then condescendingly threatened, "I'm looking forward to it."

Ramy eagerly rushed up to me the next day in class, dying to know what had happened, and was shocked at the punishment that was dished out.

Then it dawned on me, "Dude! I have to find a monologue and memorize it! I'm up in a couple-a-days!" After heading over to the shelf, and grabbing a book at random, an array of monologue options were nervously thumbed through, with the hopes of finding the shortest one possible. "What are you going to do?" Ramy asked right as I landed on a page with the shortest-looking piece; it was written in the style of Shakespeare. "There! I'll do this one!" Uncertain about my choice, Ramy gave me a side-eyed stare—"YOU'RE going to perform THAT?"

Mr. Friberg sat in the front row of the theater with a pen and notepad, watching me squirm on stage after giving the go-ahead. My lines were memorized, but how did this "acting thing" work?

WOOSH!

A sudden unexplainable burst of inspiration sucked me right into the Elizabethan era and placed me smack dab in the middle of a thick forest! To my left was a gigantic stone tower, and on its balcony was Julia (my character's love interest): she had blond braided hair wrapped around her head, and wore a royal blue gown. Hunched over on the railings, she sobbed uncontrollably—I sensed a tragic breakup!

My skin morphed into my character's while venting, self-reflecting, and screaming at the thought of losing Julia's love—a sense of pure empathy opened up inside me! The experience was sublime, and at that moment, a deep understanding of how sacred the art of acting was, sunk in... *Acting* wasn't about "acting" at all! It was about **LIVING!**

And... SCENE!

Snapping out of it, I stared out into a very silent theater—you could hear a pin drop. Then without warning, a roaring sea of applause took the entire house by storm!

Taken aback and embarrassed by all the praise, I quickly ran off the stage and sat beside an utterly shocked Ramy, who leaned in and proudly whispered, "Dude, that was *really* good!" As the applause continued, Mr. Friberg turned around in his seat, and stared at me perplexed; after a thought, he shrugged his shoulders, then turned to face the stage.

After class, Mr. Friberg commented from the sidelines as I passed by him—"You're a very good actor... But you still have detention. I'll see you after school."

While painting the ginormous backdrops for the school play, I developed a newfound respect for the theater and the collaborative environment that it bred; being a part of a community of artists provided me with one of the most unexpectedly enriching experiences at Burlingame High; it was the best punishment I could have ever had!

Thank you, Mr. Friberg!

SEVEN

KEEPIN' IT REAL

It was graduation day! There was no desire to participate in the ceremony, but my parents insisted—they hadn't worked so hard not to see their son walk. It was an emotionally charged goodbye to four incredible years— Burlingame High, Class of '99!

The plan was to attend the College of San Mateo (Jr. College), save money, then transfer to San Francisco State University as a broadcast or cinema major. My passion for entertainment took flight during my senior year of high school in Mr. Willard's video production class, having excelled in assignments like short films and directing music videos (two were played over the school's morning broadcast). So naturally, television production and filmmaking were career interests. Yet unconsciously, the love of performance continued to brew deep inside while opting for a more "logical" career path.

College was a blast, allowing me to go at a steady pace, which made me fully appreciate each subject. However, on one specific morning, the good times would come to a sudden halt with a jarring call from my cousin Lucy: "Nick, are you watching the news!? We're under attack!"

It was shocking to witness the imagery splattered all over the news. Mom and Dad walked into the living room (after my verbal reaction awakened them from their sleep) and gathered around the television set. What we had fled from in Beirut was now at our doorstep: 9/11.

A dormant childhood trauma resurfaced in unexpected and powerful ways, affecting all areas of my day-to-day life, including sleepless nights with nonstop nightmares, and being stereotyped left and right because of how the media perpetually framed and regurgitated the horrible event. Watching people be conditioned into fear and hate became disheartening. As the aura of America slowly shifted into darkness, my aspiration for producing the news soured and instead, I opted to major in cinema.

Time flew by with my transition from Jr. College, over to San Francisco State University! Simultaneously, my family was going through a transition of their own: Mom and Dad bought their very first house about two hours away from Burlingame! Mom was retired, and Dad would commute to his now shuttle management job at the car rental company *(he got promoted!)*. Mom, Dad, Janet, and Mary would move away, and I'd stay behind to start my education at San Francisco State as a nearly 23-year-old.

But where would I live?

My college buddy **Henrik** would be the answer to that prayer—*His Superpower:*

attracting any mate with his deadly combo of soft-spokenness and Val Kilmer looks. Henrik was a Dane from Denmark—we met back at community college, and coincidentally, his dad was *The Donald Trump of the Bay Area:* the man bought old properties, and rebuilt them into housing complexes.

There was one property Henrik and I had our eye on—a four-bedroom house in Burlingame that was scheduled for demolition in three years!

After convincing his dad, Henrik snagged us the spot! We moved in, brought on two other roommates, and split the rent four ways, each paying an easy $450.00 a month on Floribunda Avenue!

Teary-eyed goodbye hugs and kisses were exchanged with my family, knowing that things would never be the same again. Mom and Dad had endured so much to make a life for us, and at that moment, an overwhelming depth of gratitude opened up in me as their sacrifices sank into a sacred place in my heart. Sometimes, change can be difficult, especially for a family that has relied heavily on banding together to survive.

As Dad handed me the keys to Mom's '97 gold Toyota Corolla, a breaking away had been initiated; life would no longer be experienced under the influence of my parents. For the very first time, I'd be experiencing life on my own.

Responsibilities—*fun!* Rent! Utilities! Groceries—*lots of FUN!* My part-time job at the retail clothing store (J.CREW) wouldn't cut it if *staying alive* was a desired goal. So in came my pal Henrik to the rescue once again, with a referral to one of the hottest restaurants in town, Left At Albuquerque *(a.k.a. "Lefty's")*.

Life was rockin'—serving tables, flirting with customers, studying at San Francisco State, visiting my family every other weekend, and throwing lively house parties with Henrik at our place on alternate weekends! We spent a decent amount of time ensuring our hairstyles were spiked to perfection before opening our doors to a flood of friends and Bay Area locals—all while growing in popularity as *"The Cool Guys."*

Long gone were the days of my silly vocal impressions—it was the word *"cool"* that defined me—*COOL, I tell ya!* But, not for long...

A character voice slipped out in front of Henrik one day at our place, & the guy got such a kick out of it that he decided to throw me under the bus while at our buddy Chris' house during a get-together.

"Bro, be quiet!"

Henrik shrugged it off, "Dude, who cares? It's funny, do a voice!" It was a Friday evening, and we were all set to head out to the city with our buddies and their attractive dates. No voices for me! No way! That was last on my list of *things to do,* especially in front of girls ... because ... can you say ... *"social suicide!?"*

Too late!

Chris' interest was piqued—he darted right up from the couch, lit up like a kid on Christmas, and obnoxiously shouted, "Dude, you do voices!? No way, do one!" He was relentless—once Chris wanted something ... there was unfortunately no way of shutting him up until he got it! Reluctantly pushing back, I argued, "It's just something I did a long time ago, man"—Henrik antagonistically interjected, *"Don't lie...* You did it the other day at our place." I snapped at him—*"Dude,* SHUT UP!" He gave a careless shrug/smile combo, leaving me to fend for myself.

CHRIS' LIGHTBULB MOMENT!

"DUDE! We should prank call someone!" Our friend group was instantly on board with the idea as my stomach began to rumble, my palms started to sweat, and my heart sped up! The more our friend group (led by Chris) egged me on, the more my *talent* screamed to be let loose and play!

"FINE! One prank call, and then we all go out, okay?!"—it was my only solution to their unyielding pressure. Everyone immediately backed off and eagerly awaited their show.

What started as a prank call to a sandwich shop turned into a night of ridiculous antics: everyone was sprawled all over Chris' living room floor, dying of uncontrollable laughter, balling their eyes out, and desperately trying to regain their breathing patterns.

After composing himself, Chris experienced another lightbulb moment and screamed, "Ooh, DUDE! *Call* Mike, *call* Mike! He's at the bar now!"

The bartender handed the phone over to our buddy Mike, who answered with an *"Olay ... Olay Olay Olay...!"* (Mike was a huge soccer fan).

Our friends gathered around while I settled on a breathy, nasally female voice for Mike and whispered seductively, *"Hey... Is this Mike?"* Mike was immediately taken by the *"woman"* on the other end of the line and responded, *"Yeeeah,* who is this?" Spitting out the first name that came to mind, *"Mary"* flew out of my mouth, further intriguing Mike, as he pressed in to ask, "Mary? Mary *who?"* Our friend group covered their mouths and chuckled while my brain did cartwheels attempting to produce a darn last name!

The pub immediately came to mind: Dicey Riley's. Out of sheer desperation, I found myself hesitantly whispering, *"Uhh ... RILEY! I'm Mary! MARY RILEY!"* Chris earnestly leaned over to me and asked, *"Mary Riley? Like the Julia Roberts horror film?"* I waved him off and got back to Mike, who could be heard calling out, "Are you still there?"

It seemed that no matter how ridiculously over-the-top and cartoony "Mary" sounded, Mike wanted her all the more! He would not allow "Mary" to wrap things up—Mike wanted to know MORE about "Mary" and her interests!

What started off as a prank, quickly morphed into an uncomfortably drawn-out sensual conversation with our buddy Mike, who drunkenly begged, "Where are you right now? Waddaya into? Come on down, I'm here at the bar!"

Our prank call had backfired! So we decided to cut our losses, end the call, and leave our buddy, Mike, longing for his sweetheart, "Mary Riley" (*not* ... the Julia Roberts film).

The fun-filled night went on and on as I pretended to be everyone, from an Arab American named "Ahmed Smith" (*"Ello? I am looking for a table; vee have 20 peepel."*) to an elderly grandmother searching for her granddaughter at a TGI FRIDAYS restaurant in San Mateo.

The bartender answered the call to hear a crackly elderly woman's voice obnoxiously calling out, *"HELLO!?? I'm looking for my granddaughter ... Joanna...* (a name I thought up at random) *Is she there?"* The bartender placed me on hold, and about two minutes later, a lovely woman got on the line and asked, "Hello, are you looking for the big group at the bar?"

We were all caught off guard; who did the bartender hand the phone over to?

Treading cautiously, I stayed in character, and loudly repeated, *"I'm looking for my granddaughter, Joanna. Is this... JO-Annnn-AH?"* Wanting clarity on the name, the woman asked, "Who?" I condescendingly reiterated and overly pronounced, *"JowwwAAAnnnAH."*

The woman's tone indicated surprise and confusion ... because ... she **WAS** JOANNA! She trepidatiously answered, "Yeah, it is..."

We were SHELL-SHOCKED! Our friend group burst into laughter as I immediately hung up, disturbed, at what seemed like a well-orchestrated coincidence! She was there in the flesh ... at TGI FRIDAY'S ... **"JOANNA!"**

After everyone settled down, Chris received a sudden burst of inspiration—

"DUDE! YOU SHOULD DO VOICES FOR VIDEO GAMES AND CARTOONS!"—another one of Chris' lightbulb moments. Our entire friend group agreed, and to hear this kind of encouragement from my peers meant the world! Chris' uncompromising belief in my ability to *"do voices"* on a professional scale planted a powerful seed that night. It made me wholeheartedly believe that I would, in fact, successfully fulfill his prophetic advice!

I DO VOICES

I called every voice-over studio in San Francisco and offered to intern for them. One called me back—a V.O. (voice-over) production house and school, owned and operated by Elaine Clark. She offered this deal: in exchange for running errands and tidying up her studio between workshops, she would grant me college credit and allow me to take entry-level voice-over workshops free of charge. The more advanced classes

would be discounted at a whopping 50% off—
fair enough!

Eileen, the motherly office manager, walked up to me one day and timidly relayed, "I'm so sorry to ask you to do this, Nick, but Elaine would like you to tidy up the bathroom before the next class." Eileen was a beautiful blond-haired, blue-eyed gal who could still turn heads, even in her mature age. My reaction was a careless shrug and an, "Okay, cool." Mom always had us tidy up the house before guests came over, so this request wasn't that big of a deal.

About 45 minutes into my cleaning spree, Eileen knocked on the bathroom door and asked concernedly, "Nick, are you doing okay in there?" She nudged the door open, bumped me in the behind, and looked down to find me on my knees, wearing cleaning gloves, while scrubbing around the toilet with cleaning powder. Eileen's eyes went wide in shock as she exclaimed, "Oh my gosh, Nick, I didn't mean for you to clean the entire bathroom! I just meant, replace the toilet paper and wipe down the sink!" Staring up at her nonchalantly, my deadpan response was, "Yeah but this is how my mom tidies up." Eileen was at a loss for words and regretfully affirmed, "Hold on, I'll be right back."

Moments later, Eileen came back to relay this message: "I just told Elaine what you did, and she wants you to know that you can take all the classes here for free."

During the internship, over $7,000.00 worth of voice-over workshops were taken by yours truly!

My vocal range EXPANDED to extremes, as I fell madly in love with voice-acting! A voice-over demo (characters and commercials) was produced using the built-in mic on my G3 iMac, and it was so rinky-dinky, but it did the job! There was no stopping me; I HAD to become a voice actor! After all, my buddy Chris said so! Remembering his *"You should do voices..."* advice, SEGA immediately popped into my mind! Their giant emblem was at the top of a tall brick building in San Francisco, right next to where Mom used to work! It was time to be *"Agent Nick"* and pitch myself to SEGA!

A snarky receptionist who sounded bored with life answered the phone and heard an earful—"Hi, my name is Nick Shakoour, and I'm a voice actor. What's the best way to be considered for auditions?" The receptionist subtly retaliated, "We don't cast voices for our games here. It's a different company that does that for us".

It was time to be *"Inspector Nick"* and ask, "Well, can you tell me the name of the company that *does* cast the voices?" There was a brief silence, then a begrudgingly stated, "Webtone." I thanked the receptionist, she hung up the call without saying another word, and I ... got a LEAD!

My voice-over demo C.D. was mailed to Webtone the very next day, and shortly after, the nonstop follow-up calls would commence! Greg Weber (owner of Webtone) graciously took my call weekly to hear me ask the same question: "Hi, Mr. Weber, have you had a chance to listen to my voice-over demo yet?" Greg would repeatedly say, "I'm busy right now. Call me back next week."

As the *Pester Greg* cycle ran rampant, week after week, month after month, call after call, I drove the guy nuts: "Hey, Mr. Weber, it's Nick! Have you had a chance to listen to my voice-over demo?" Greg got super irritated on one of the calls and annoyedly begged, "STOP calling me *'MR. Weber!'* It's **'GREG!'** And NO! Check back next week!"

Next week later...

"Hey Mr. Weber—*er*, I mean *Greg*, how are you doing? It's Nick, and I'm wondering if you had a chance to listen to my voice demo?"

Greg's wife (and business partner) would also answer the phone periodically, and by the one-millionth call, she interrupted my *autopilot introduction* explaining, "Nick, I know it's you, honey; I'm sorry he's just really busy." A frustrated Greg could be heard calling out to his wife from a distance, "Who is it?!" She yelled back, "It's Nick! The kid just wants a job!" Greg got on the line right away and aggressively asked, "Are you available to come in tomorrow for an audition?" I jumped for joy and yelled, "YES!"

My heart was pounding as I pulled into the parking lot of Webtone in my gold Toyota Corolla! After being buzzed in by Greg's wife, she had me wait in the lobby for Greg, where I sat looking around, thinking, *"This is so freaking cool! I'm about to audition for video games!"*

Greg's frantic entrance caught my attention; he was a green-eyed, mustached man who looked like he was zapped right out of the '80s! I eagerly stood up out of my chair, held out my hand, and in response, Greg slammed a stack of scripts down onto the coffee table, pointed right at me, and combatively ordered, "You've got ten minutes! I'll be back to get you!"

Flipping through each script was paradise, as monsters, warriors, and an ancient tree came to life before my eyes, transforming me into their very being! Time ceased to exist while joyously trying them on for size.

Ten minutes on the dot, Greg came marching back into the lobby and impatiently asked, "Ready?"

As I eagerly stood inside a high-tech voice-over booth, Greg stared on in confusion at my childlike wonder from the other side of the soundproof glass. After a moment of bewildered frustration, he leaned over to the communication button, pressed it, and impatiently asked, "So, how do you want to do this? Do you want to take breaks between each character, or do you want to go through them all at once?" My joyously careless answer was, "Yeah sure, I can do all of them back to back that's good!" Greg shook his head, aggressively hit the record button, and, in defeat, surrendered with, "Okay, whenever you're ready."

A PARTY erupted inside of that booth! Rapidly going from one script to the next, every character was devoured like a ravenous wolf! After flipping over the final script, lots of heavy panting took place, paired with slight dizziness—*what a rollercoaster ride!*

After coming to, I looked up to find Greg frozen, with his mouth gaped open. He cautiously leaned over to his left, gently pressed the communication button, and confessed, "I am so sorry for having blown you off for all these months. From now on, you will audition for every game I ever cast and direct—you can do any character!"

Greg loved himself some baseball, and he used this analogy: "You know who you're like? You're like that guy who's never played ball but knows how to hold the bat, do the swing, and instinctively hit a home run! That's YOU! You've never done this before?" My response— "I've done prank calls."

Some *really* cool games were booked through Webtone, including *Shining Tears* as the lead superhero, *Armored Core* as military fighters, and *Otogi 2* as the 10,000-year-old tree named Sutake, to name a few. My life was FULL: college courses were being aced, serving tables was a blast, throwing house parties with my buddies grew in tradition, visiting my family every other weekend for love bombs commenced, interning at the voice-over studio inspired professionalism, and work was being booked as a voice actor! Things could not have gotten any better... *Or so I thought.*

EIGHT

IS THIS LOVE?

I had an amazing summer internship at a film production house in Los Angeles right before going into my senior year at San Francisco State. After tasting the excitement of LA, defaulting back to my easygoing hometown of Burlingame left me yearning for more: things that once pleased me ... no longer satisfied.

One evening, Henrik barged into the living room, inviting me to a house party, but I shot the guy down. He pushed back arguing, "Come on man, don't be lame. Just come."

After reluctantly asking him whose house party it was, Henrik revealed, "It's a new friend I made on campus today. His name is also *Nick—he's Greek like you, I think.*"

I really didn't feel like going, but then I thought, *"How could anyone not go to a party being thrown by 'Nick?'"*

OPA!

The place was Greeked-out to the max, with dance music, a plethora of food, and an overflow of drinks! Positivity filled the air as Henrik briefly introduced me to that *Nick* guy who was hosting the entire thing, and he wasn't the only *"Nick"* there. Because the gathering consisted mainly of Bay Area Greeks, you could spot a *"Nick"* everywhere. At one point in the evening, while standing with a group of guys conversing, someone called out, "HEY NICK!" and we all turned.

Later on that night...

While lounging around in the kitchen with Henrik, casually scoping out the variety of partiers, a mysterious girl came into focus: she had wavy caramel-colored hair and the most mesmerizing eyes to match. As I found myself obsessively zeroing in on her, everything else began to fade away. She gently flung her hair back and revealed the most genuine smile. Leaning over to Henrik, I pointed out, "Dude, look at that girl. She's beautiful." Henrik suggested, "You should go talk to her." Snapping out of my momentary infatuation, my interest was retracted with a playful, "Naw she looks like a b****"—*naughty Nick.*

Throughout the night, the mystery girl and I had constant *bump-ins.* On about our third one, my smart aleck remark suggested, "We gotta stop meeting like this." She unabashedly laughed, and we connected instantly, eventually dancing together in the living room.

Yelling over the loud music, I commented, "You know we're the only ones dancing, right!?" She shouted back, "They're all going to think we're dorks!" To which I shrugged off a "Let them!"

Our conversation and connection kept flowing as we began to fall under each other's spell. The verbal communication eventually ceased as we became transfixed ... silently stared into each other's eyes ... and moved in closer to ...

"HEY EVERYONE! The neighbors said they're going to call the cops if we don't end the party! All of you have to GO!"—leave it up to *"Nick"* to ruin a moment. Not this *"Nick"* (the one writing the book)—the owner of the house *"Nick."* Dang it, NICK!

His abrupt announcement jarred us from a deepening connection and brought our surroundings back into focus as a crowd of semi-drunk college kids stampeded their way past us like wildebeests!

Turning my attention back to the mystery girl—she was gone! As I searched for her, Henrik rushed over urging, "Come on, man, let's go!"

Over there!

The mystery girl was heading to the front door, accompanied by her two girlfriends—they shielded her from an onslaught of lustfully drunken college guys—"Hey! Hey! Let me get your number!" "Yo, let me get that number!"

Following closely behind with Henrik, I yelled, "Why don't you guys leave her alone!? She isn't interested!" The drunken dudes immediately scattered off as the mystery girl came to a complete stop, turning to see that it was me, the guy she'd been dancing with.

Intrigued, she asked, "Why aren't *you* asking for my number?" I nonchalantly responded, "You obviously don't want to give it out, so why would I ask for it?" Her interest was piqued as she playfully suggested, "Well ... why don't you ask me for it, and maybe I'll give it to you."

In hindsight, if I could have gone back in time to prevent the number exchange from ever happening, I would have!
My nearly 24-year-old self had no idea the world of hurt he was about to enter: this girl was kryptonite in disguise.

Now, back to the story...
(Don't do it, Nick! Don't do it!!!)
I ended up asking her for her number.
(Oy vey Nick!)

What started as an ice cream date in San Francisco transformed into a flourishing relationship within months. We GOT each other; it was the first time the thought of commitment, or the potential for marriage, had ever floated around in my mind! She was wife material, and one night during an intimate embrace, a deeply heartfelt "I love you" surprisingly slipped out of me; she was just as shocked, touched, and could only muster up, "Oh babe." Her unsure response made for one awkward moment—*talk about leaving a guy hanging.*

The *I-love-yous* eventually started pouring out on her end, and we couldn't get enough of each other; our constant hangouts piqued her parents' interest in meeting me—at first there was major hesitation on my part, not wanting to deal with unnecessary pressure or premature expectations. Still, the girlfriend begged, and I gave in. *Why?* Because you know... "I love you."

*Upon arriving at my girlfriend's
enchanted kingdom, her pristine
house could be seen nestled on top of
a luscious green hillside in what seemed like
a hidden part of the world; it was where
the who's who of who's who lived.
Meanwhile, I was sporting shorts, flip-flops,
a snug T-shirt, & ... my overly spiked hair.*

THEY. DID. NOT. LIKE. ME. ONE. BIT.

Or my spiked hair for that matter. We can't forget about my *six o'clock shadow...* Ooh, they HATED that too! *Stubble*—YUCK! My carefree, boisterous persona seemed to have clashed with her parents' ultra-reserved and standoffish, *we're better than thou* demeanor. They couldn't figure me out for the life of them and turned their noses up at me like I was the equivalent of trash. After all, I *was* majoring in cinema while pursuing voice acting for a living. *Translation—"You're a NOBODY."* Soon enough, this extreme clash of opposing worlds would drive a painful wedge within our sacred relationship.

WE BROKE UP

Yup ... that sure was fast! My girlfriend broke up with me over the phone—just like that. She and her parents had been breaking out into arguments over little ol' me, and she couldn't do it anymore. My heart winced with uncontrollable pain as complete and utter shock knocked me off course, making me lose sight of myself.

The situation was exacerbated by the fact that we, as a couple, never had any issues; my girlfriend was trapped with one foot in a life of privilege and the other in pauper land with me—a choice had to be made.

About an hour later, guttural screams and an overflow of weeping in the fetal position on the pavement of my ex-girlfriend's driveway overtook my sensibilities—all while her mom stood there, watching through the window (I'm sure she enjoyed the show). The girlfriend wanted to say goodbye in person, so like an idiot, I commuted over to her.

Gutted and completely drained of my *Superpower*, I slowly got up, shuffled over to my Toyota Corolla, and drove away from her enchanted kingdom.

A mixture of surprisingly volatile emotions erupted left and right; I had officially lost sight of my *true* self—the *real* me. Our relationship led me to believe that if it didn't exist, I didn't exist. It defined itself as being *"crucial"* for *my* survival—*utter nonsense*—but I fell for the trick!

Mom and Dad came to my rescue to the best of their abilities, but it was new territory for them, too. They did their best to relieve me of the effects of *kryptonite,* but it was no use. While riding in the car with Dad, he advised, "If she calls you, don't respond immediately! Watch, she's going to be sorry for what she did." Not a moment later, the ex was calling, but I let it go to voicemail. She left a snarky-sounding message saying, "Hey, it's me. I've been thinking about things, and we shouldn't break up because of my parents. So if you WANT to get back together, let me know." She oozed entitlement, and her lack of humility or remorse *po'd* me off!

If I just had that time machine
to stop myself from returning her stupid call,
life would have been much simpler
& way less stupid. But admittedly,
it wouldn't have been as interesting.

Now, let's proceed, shall we...?
(Don't do it, Nick! Please don't do it!!!)
I ended up returning her call.
(Oy vey Nick!)

Things were never the same after we got back together; the open and honest relationship was gone and, instead, was replaced with undercurrents of resentment, paranoia, and deep hurt. Taking her back was almost like a form of self-betrayal—wholeness couldn't be felt without her. Where was my dignity? Where was my self-worth? I swore never to give 100% of myself ever again! We should have let go of the relationship but *codependency* was KING—*how could we have said goodbye?*

To make matters worse, her family did a fantastic job of making me feel completely worthless as she joined in on the *Demean Nick Fest* in hopes of motivating me to become what her parents wanted me to be: wealthy and successful, someone they could present to their social circles as "worthy."

Her parents would eventually accomplish their ultimate goal: Eradicate the Relationship & Crush Nick's Spirit.

My girlfriend and I fought desperately to get back to how we used to be, but life's circumstances kept pulling us apart. After graduating from SF State, I tried like a madman to make a film career happen in the Bay Area for a solid year, to no avail! These nutjobs wanted me to either work for free or do low-paying, super part-time work—I couldn't catch a break!

I needed a full-time thing that PAID! There was a very anxious girlfriend desperately awaiting my financial success! Her "motivational" advice was constantly repeated in my mind: "They (her parents) just want to see you do more. They don't see anything happening with your career!" My efforts were always shrugged off, no matter the achievement. Anxiety, exhaustion, and depression took over, trying to please a family who were only interested in two things: money and status, and I ... had neither.

After multiple failed attempts at a filmmaking career in the Bay Area, I decided to stick to my post-graduation plan & move to Los Angeles.

The next four years of my life became a circus act: taking photos of background actors at an extra's casting office (the only real work I could get in LA), hounding top V.O. agencies for representation (they all shot me down), and commuting up north once a month for family and girlfriend visits. My move to LA would be the final nail in the coffin for us.

Gone were the days of openly talking about marriage, as almost every conversation led to verbal blows induced by the constant pressure from her parents. As a fun side note ... her mom had been setting her up on dates with eligible bachelors to get her to lose interest in me. *Fun times!* My girlfriend agreed to go on one "innocent" lunch date to get her mom off her back. It was understandable because her family knew his family ... and it would have been rude not to—*so thoughtful.* I was shoved into a pressure cooker and was about to explode!

Four years into our rocky relationship, my girlfriend invited me to an outdoor holiday event in the Bay Area. Mom went in my place since I couldn't afford to make two trips up north in a single month.

With the constant stress hanging over our relationship, my girlfriend and I didn't want to face the ugly truth... We were both over it.

Christmas Eve ... a time for family, friends, and headaches! I was at my parents' house, surrounded by family, including my soon-to-be brother-in-law Gabriel and his mom and brother.

The girlfriend and her parents were out of town for the holidays, so it was a huge relief not having to endure their *we don't want you here* stares.

While my family opened presents (we opened gifts on Christmas Eve), a nudge was sensed to do the *good boyfriend thing* and at least give my girlfriend a call. There was tension in the air, and maybe things could be smoothed over, but it was a no-go; her tone indicated indifference right off the bat. Feeling disrespected and annoyed, I cut things short and returned to the living room frustrated.

"What am I going to do, Mom!? She wants me to change, and it feels like I'm having to kill off who I am for her parents!" Mom paused, then looked at me and advised, "It sounds like you'll have to if you feel like you can't live without her."

Mom didn't want to say what she was about to say as she revealed, "Remember her Christmas event I went to in your place? Your girlfriend's mom and her friend were there too. They looked down on me arrogantly while her mom's friend condescendingly asked, 'Is your son STILL trying to be a filmmaker?' Then, they both laughed at me."

I CRACKED!

Marching right back into our guest room, the girlfriend was called up, and Mom's story was thrown right in her face! While hurling hurtful insults at her and her family, I wouldn't allow her to get a word in edgewise!

Tolerating years of mind games while unjustifiably being treated like dirt, drove me over the edge, and as my rage erupted like a volcano, I screamed, "LET'S JUST BREAK UP!"

She was unresponsive ... silence on the other end of the line—"Hello?" My girlfriend softly chimed in with a simple, "Fine." Her agreeable response to my empty threat was unexpected and made me wonder if she was listening: "I'm breaking up with you! Did you hear me?!" She responded with a dismally soft-spoken, "Okay." In a last-ditch effort, I threatened, "We are NEVER getting back together AGAIN!" She calmly reassured, "That's fine."

Our relationship was over that night, and Christmas ... became my most hated holiday.

NINE

RASHEED DOES NOT DRINK PROTEIN!

NEW YEAR, newly single me! The relationship from the pit of hell had ended—*woo-hoo!* While unconsciously compressing the post-breakup hurt into a tight ball of denial, my focus was diverted to making a V.O. / filmmaking career happen! Unbeknownst to me, a rare opportunity was about to fall right into my lap while sitting at my desk, editing a photo of a background actor at the extras casting job.

Boss Lady strolled up and asked, "Hey, um, Nick, you speak Arabic, right?" My response: "Yeah, but it's Lebanese Arabic, what's up?"

Two female actresses were selected for a final callback on a documentary-style war film that Boss Lady's Casting Director friend was working on, and they needed an Iraqi speaker to help. Clarifying that Iraqi Arabic wasn't in my wheelhouse didn't seem to pose an issue. Casting deemed it sufficient, and I found myself in a house garage converted into a full production suite in Santa Monica, CA.

The place was decked out with pro lights, cameras, and editing bays; did the Apple Store and IKEA have an illegitimate child no one knew about? Casting introduced me to the director, who, for the sake of this book, we'll call "Michael Mopfield." He was from London and spoke with what sounded like a permanently whiny sore throat. Mopfield looked at you in an "I pity your existence" way.

"Theeea's the *maaattress* on the *flooooor,"* Mopfield whined, with his elongated, English accent. *"Weird,"* I thought.

Cut to a few moments later, and Casting was on the couch, sandwiched between Mopfield and his overly eager camera operator, and there I was, lying down on the mattress, waiting for my "wife." The breakup had rendered me fearless, so shyness was out the window!

Sudden unease took the room by storm, however, as the first actress shuffled in; she had to lovingly wake me in a panic after spotting someone plant an explosive outside our "window," but the chemistry was just off. It sucked big time! Instead of connecting with yours truly, she was more invested in proving herself in the role—wailing and screaming uncontrollably to the point of my experiencing second-hand embarrassment!

Once the scene ended, she was thanked for coming in and left oozing with desperation— I felt so bad for her! Casting turned to Mopfield nervously and hesitantly nodded while affirming, "She was good...?" Mopfield looked away, stared into space, and disappointedly announced to the room, "She's too *ooowld* and she's too *faaat*." My jaw dropped!

The atmosphere immediately shifted into *fun* with the next actress, who shuffled in all giddy and childlike; she was a big kid at heart, open and ready to play! She let out a radiant smile reminiscent of my ex's, and right off the bat, there was chemistry!

Passion took us by storm as we improvised the same bedroom scene—it felt like we were husband and wife! The entire room disappeared as we became one with the story, with each other, and everyone watching. We panicked, flirted, and even kissed as my desperate longing for a relationship manifested via my connection to this actress!

"*CAUUUT!*" was called by Mopfield; his face—beaming with pride. Everyone sat frozen on the couch as Mopfield reacted, "*Waaaow ... that was greeeat.*" The actress hugged me tightly, joyously thanked everyone, and effortlessly skipped off.

Mopfield turned his attention back to me and just stared ... FOREVER. He then complimented, "You were *greeeat.*" The statement threw me off—I wasn't acting.

Back at my job, Boss Lady wanted to have a word. *"What did I do wrong?"* was on mental repeat while slowly opening her office door to find her seated at her desk, smirking, with her phone receiver in hand. Boss Lady asked, "Nick, what did you do at that audition?" Quickly panicking while recalling my kissy-kissy time with that actress, DEFENSE MODE was activated—"Look, I didn't mean to kiss her, it just happened!" Boss Lady shook her head, chuckled, offered me the receiver, and revealed, "Casting is on the phone for you."

Slowly placing the phone to my ear while cautiously bracing myself for the worst, Casting's delighted tone caught me by surprise—she wasn't mad at all!

"Hey, Nick! Thank you so much for helping me out today! By the way, Mopfield LOVED your performance!" Again... *"What performance?"* Then she asked, "What are you doing for the next three months?" A spine-tingling chill ran down my back as Casting let her rip; "Mopfield believed you as the husband so much so that he just fired the guy he originally hired to play Rasheed, and he wants to cast you instead!"

My brain immediately did backflips! *Was a supporting lead being offered to ME?* A mixture of deeply buried emotions bubbled to the surface as the moment flew right in the face of the mental narrative my ex's parents had fabricated for my life! I WAS worth something, after all!

Casting clarified, "Look, you don't have to give me an answer right away. Take a day or two and think about it. The film shoots for three months in Jordan, and you'll need to get a passport."

This was all happening way too fast! Without saying another word to Casting, I somberly handed the phone back to Boss

Lady, quietly excused myself, and left the building.

Standing under the warm LA sun, I looked up into the sky and burst into tears. Someone had seen value in me.

JORDAN BABY!

My family was stoked—especially Mom! What a crazy turn of events! Mopfield and his producers put us up in the 2000-year-old city of Jerash, and because his ongoing theme for his film (à la his English accent) was, "I *wont* (want) it to be *reeeal,*" living in my character's home along with my on-screen wife, was a must—I was now set to play Rasheed!

Two suitcases filled with two five-pound tubs of chocolate protein powder; that's what was brought with me to Jordan. Weight lifting and nutrition were my obsessions post-breakup, and commitment to the *muscle bro cause* was a must! But you know who disapproved? Mopfield: his "I *wont* it to be *reeeal*" philosophy was the priority, and anything or anyone that threatened his ironclad vision would send him flying off the rails—an automatic switch had gone off making him super volatile and outright *cuckoo!*

Mopfield wanted us to live, think, and dress like our characters, 24/7. Even on our off days, I kid you not! Not only were we expected to live in our character's home, but we also had to stay in their wardrobe because ... "I *wont* it to be *reeeal.*" Mopfield would chew us out if we didn't! He'd ambush us on our days off with his crew to see if we were *living in character.* Like I said—*cuckoo!*

Mopfield would scream at the top of his lungs if he caught us doing anything besides what he thought our characters should be doing. Once, we asked for takeout, and Mopfield told us we'd have to buy and kill a real chicken! We just wanted dinner—*cuckoo!* He never bothered to give us a character breakdown to help guide us on what not to do in the first place! *Insanity-Ville! Cuckoo!*

Everything seemed to piss Mopfield off. Even my incessant need to ingest protein shakes! That's right... A simple run-of-the-mill protein shake is what finally pushed Mopfield over the edge as he screamed out in agony, "RASHEED DOES NOT DRINK PROTEIN!!!" Mopfield took a beat, remembered something else he couldn't stand, and shouted, "... STOP DOING PUSH-UPS! RASHEED DOES NOT DO PUSH-UPS!" I had been secretly doing push-ups in between setups... *Oops—cuckoo!*

I quit protein for the duration of what would be a film shoot from hell, and got right down to business filming scenes with that bubbly actress from the audition; she ended up getting the part! We successfully improvised one scene after the next, while everyone, including hard-to-please Mopfield, enjoyed our performances. But there was one ***teeny-tiny*** problem—*my dialect:* Lebanese Arabic ... in a film that required an Iraqi speaker—**uh-oh!**

Remember when production got the heads-up about my not knowing how to speak Iraqi Arabic? The dialogue in this film would be completely improvised using a general scene outline, and there'd be no way of writing or memorizing any set of lines. When initially offered the role, Casting reassured me that production would be willing to work with me on the "accent." Now, unfortunately, we weren't dealing with an accent here—we were dealing with a full-blown dialect! One that I knew diddly-squat about!

Mopfield came up with a brilliant plan! He would trap me in a hotel with four Iraqi translators for one week, thereby forcing me to magically learn Iraqi Arabic, a language I'd never spoken—*cuckoo!* Mopfield threatened, "If you *caun't* speak *Iraauqi,* then I'm *soarrry* ... you *caun't* be *Rasheeed."* Throat lump—*yikes!* That was motivation enough to go along with this outlandishly impossible plan.

But hey ... after one week of *Iraqi Dialect Boot Camp,* I was utterly fluent in a language I'd never spoken—Iraqi! Not too shabby, huh? *Yeah right*—I WISH! I was more fluent in butchering the language than speaking it by the end of the seven days!

While filming scenes, small pieces of paper would desperately be hidden up my sleeve with general Iraqi phrases written all over them. The entire shoot was a disaster: the actress would deliver an emotionally charged line in Iraqi Arabic, and in turn, I'd respond with the first generic phrase that I could catch a glimpse of. The actress and on-set translators were thrown for a loop!

AMBUSH!

Mopfield and his crew ganged up on me one somber morning for a surprise meeting as he seemingly switched between two dueling personas: *Sweet* Mopfield and *Mean* Mopfield.

Strangely enough, while mostly directing his dialogue to the floor (and not at me), *Sweet* Mopfield appeared and softly relayed, "The translators on set *aaar* telling me *yoer* having trouble speaking *Iraauqi*." I thought, "DUH!" He added, "Look, we think *yoer greeeat.* We even thought, 'Hey ... maybe Rasheed *COULD* be Lebanese...'"

Then, without warning, *Mean* Mopfield overtook *Sweet* Mopfield as he pouted like a child and abruptly retaliated, "But NO! Rasheed is *NAUT* Lebanese! He's *Iraauqi*! HE SPEAKS *IRAAUQI*!"

I thought, *"Sheesh ... chill, bro, no one's arguing with you on this!"* After pulling himself together, *Sweet* Mopfield reemerged, looked up at me with his puppy dog eyes, and regretfully concluded, "I'm *soarrry* ... you *caun't* be *Rasheeed.*"

DEVASTATED!

What would I tell Boss Lady back in LA!? What would I tell my family and friends!? My newfound self-worth was so deeply rooted in the role of Rasheed that the thought of being torn away from it was unthinkable! What was worse—my ex and her parents would be proven right about my never becoming anything in life! After desperately asking *Sweet* Mopfield, "Are you going to send me back home?"—he paused, contemplated my fate, and as if being told by his mom to go clean his room, whined out a regretful, *"Nooooo,* I don't *wont* to do *thaaaaat...* You're *REEEEEEALLY GOOOOD!"*

Mopfield was then hit with another one of his brilliant ideas, as he nonchalantly offered up this simple solution: "We'll just make you one of the Marines, and you can go stay with them in the barracks."

Don't worry, it gets worse...

To give you some context, there was an extensive nationwide search to cast twelve former U.S. Marines alongside guys who had been in the Army. Mopfield wanted dudes with real-life Military experience so that— you know... "I *wont* it to be *reeeal.*" These guys were vetted through a meticulous casting call to ensure they each brought something unique to their role. I had never been a Marine, never played one, and was about to be thrown into a situation that would eventually break me.

"Rasheed" was awesome—losing the role was a harsh blow to my fragile state of mind post-breakup. To make matters worse, the actress playing my wife suddenly cut off any interest in communicating with me altogether once the role was taken away. The "friendship" we formed seemed like an act, and suddenly, I was nonexistent to her; oddly enough, it felt like another real-life breakup!

What seemed like an ideal situation that would eventually help me move on, ended up widening my unconsciously traumatized cracks to the point of a full-on breakdown.

OORAH!

Thrown into the lion's den of the barracks, I rubbed shoulders with some of the most rough-and-tumble guys ever! The lead Marines were expected to treat the rest of us as real recruits, which meant borderline mental and physical abuse around the clock, even on our off days. And why? Let's all say it together now and with an English accent ... "I *wont* it to be *reeeal.*"

What a nightmare!

It was thirteen of us in a sardine-sized can of a barrack! We made home-cooked meals together ... showered together ... and I hated every second of it! There were moments of light-hearted banter, but it was a very stressful situation with constant outbursts of being belittled around the clock! This was not what I had signed up for, especially with my self-worth already being at *zero!*

It was a struggle keeping up with weapons handling and military drills: training became super intense as Mopfield constantly threatened to fire me at every turn if I didn't shape up. Hell! Utter hell! But ... I wasn't a quitter! Although throwing in the towel was an enticing idea, a small part of me admired what these former Military men had been through, and to my surprise, a friendship would be formed with one of them.

ERIC "MEHA"

Eric Mehalacopoulos (Greek translation— *Arc Angel Michael the Protector*). Eric was a former U.S. Sergeant and a French Canadian Greek; he wasn't the *fame-seeking actor type;* he was just a *dude,* and that's why we clicked. At first, Eric watched me struggle from a distance, but after getting to know me, he opened up to allow a connection between us.

Eric was nonjudgmental and trustworthy, a man of principle. But trust me, you did not EVER want to cross him—**EVER!** He was the walking definition of what the Marines called a "Devil Dog," yet there was a genuine caring heart underneath the man who was ready to snap anyone's neck at the drop of a hat *(and could)*.

Eric showed me the ropes in rifle handling, Marine terminology, and codes of conduct, as others laughed at my failures. He ran me through drills on our days off when he didn't have to. Eric had my back, and it was a good thing that he did because things were about to go from *cuckoo* ... to **certain death!**

A brilliant idea popped into Mopfield's mind (yes, another one) while scouting a neighborhood—an idea so brilliant that it nearly cost us our lives. Mopfield would casually "direct" some of the more seasoned Marines into a house that he hand-selected at random. That's right folks ... a *real* house with *real* people living inside. Now, did any of us know that? Of course, we didn't. Did the people in the house know they were about to be ambushed? Of course, *they* didn't. Now how would, "I *wont* it to be *reeeal*" happen if we all did?

Mopfield yelled, *"Aaauction!"*

The Marines violently kicked down the door of the randomly selected house with full force and charged through it screaming, with guns blazing (shooting blanks) while tossing smoke bombs left and right—*ya gotta have smoke bombs when you're clearing a house, you know?*

Mopfield yelled, *"Caaaut!"* and the guys came marching right out—they were followed by a man who was screaming in a panicked rage!

After hustling over to let him know the scene was over, the angry man violently shoved me in the chest with both arms, got in my face, and screamed, "Do I look like an actor to you!?"

Did he just say what I think he just said?

The angry man screamed, "I'm in my house, my wife is in her bra with no head covering—the next thing we know, American soldiers come in firing their guns! Go back to your country and leave us alone!"

I nearly vomited.

After a brief moment, the angry man got an idea and matter-of-factly stated, "I'm going to go back into my house (whew, thank God), grab my gun (didn't like the sound of that), and kill all of you!" (I almost went in my pants!).

My plea:

"Woah woah woah, wait a second now! I'm so sorry this happened to you and your wife—these guys are just actors! They're not real Marines! It's the director's fault! He's the crazy one who made them all do it! See the cameras?! We're just filming a movie!"

The angry man agreed that if his and his wife's honor were restored, he wouldn't kill us. And that, to me, sounded like a great alternative to murder, so I publicly humiliated Mopfield and let everyone around us know what he had just done. The Marines were *PISSED*—one guy even flung his helmet to the ground!

Production ended up compensating the angry man for the inconvenience, the Marines refused to break into anymore randomly selected houses, and yours truly ended up on Mopfield's poop list because on that one magical day, yours truly ruined ... "I *wont* it to be *reeeal!*"

UP NEXT...
A JOYRIDE!
IN A RUNAWAY HUMVEE!

Our Humvee had brake issues and exposed wiring that crackled and sparkled like the Fourth of July! After continually expressing our concerns, we were told, "Stop complaining!" Mopfield had become so madly obsessed with wanting everything to be so *"reeeal"* that we genuinely felt he was banking on some tragic event to occur so that he could capture it on film!

The guys and I suddenly found ourselves uncontrollably swerving off course onto the grassy knoll (under the rain) and accelerating toward a two-story hillside drop! Our driver pushed down on the brake pedal of the Humvee multiple times, and wouldn't you know it, the brakes gave out! He then tried steering us to safety, but the wheel locked! Everything went super slow motion while

I rode in the back seat as the other guys in the vehicle froze in shock!

Suddenly, an unexpected surge of protective power filled my entire body, transforming me into a Marine—I became fearless! With full command, I barked, "Hey guys! Come on! We *gotta* get out of here!" But they wouldn't budge!

Refusing to die on a Mopfield production, I aggressively kicked the passenger door open, crossed my arms, and launched myself backward out of the vehicle GI-Joe style!

After a rough landing, I quickly sat up to watch my brothers-in-arms race to the cliff's edge! As the Humvee reached the drop-off point, the brakes suddenly kicked in and the vehicle abruptly stopped!

Rushing over to the Humvee, my scream for evacuation snapped the guys out of it and they immediately exited the vehicle! Thank God!

There could have been some major loss that day, but luckily everything worked out! Well ... at least for us guys anyway. You see, it was a rather unfortunate day for Mopfield: his cameras had failed to capture this award-winning action-packed, "I *wont* it to be *reeeal*" moment.

The entire experience was *cuckoo,* to say the least, but it did provide me with military experience, and a friend was found in Eric, so it wasn't all bad. After three months of madness, it would finally be time to go home and rest! However, unbeknownst to me, I'd be leaving behind one kind of battle, only to face another. One ... that would be fought in my mind.

TEN

FALLEN

Mom picked me up at LAX Airport, and what a relief it was to see her after having been away for months (which is a long time by our standards). She returned to Northern California after we hung out for a few days, and then ... the dust began to settle as heaviness started to creep in: the buried shambles of my past were about to break out and destroy me.

PTSD: not having dealt with the reality of the breakup, paired with three months of madness in Jordan, left me in an unexplainable funk—*a frightening void grew deep inside.*

Moping around the apartment aimlessly became the norm, and uncertainty ... the standard: a thick heavy cloud of fear and confusion formed all around and sucked me right in!

My roommate at the time even asked, "What's going on with you, man?" His question brought something to the forefront ... the loss of my *true* identity.

Convincing myself that the breakup was somehow temporary created a false expectation in my mind while filming in Jordan. Now that there was time to sit and reflect, major realizations hit all at once: her lackluster responses over the phone on Christmas Eve were red flags—she had been instigating arguments months prior in hopes of ending the relationship—she was over it. To add insult to injury, there was a new guy at her church she'd been hanging out with who was, *"... just a friend."*

There was no more denying it ... our relationship was OVER. I felt low and insecure, but most of all ... UTTERLY STUPID for ever having gone back to her in the first place and for having allowed her parents to demean me—years of my life ... wasted!

Feeling powerless and crushed beyond comprehension, I lost complete sight of what remained of myself and plunged headfirst ... into depression.

Darkness ravaged my world, & seeing straight was impossible.
It was like being trapped in a dirty sewer tunnel, unable to find a way out.

Life lost its meaning. That once fun-loving guy named "Nick" was traded in for a mentally abusive relationship that had ripped him away from his *true* identity and depleted him of his *Superpower*—he had become a shell of his former self with feelings of unbearable existence the moment he woke up in the mornings to face the darkness.

Life sucked!

Every night, for a year straight, this was my prayer: "God, please take my soul; I can't do this anymore." Friends and family offered good advice, but it was useless—*the nightmare of my mind had me on lockdown!*

Grandpa.
The memory of you was my only hope;
you were the single thread of light
that I could grasp onto as everything
around me went pitch black...
You were my tether to God.

Connecting with the memory of Grandpa instilled a sliver of hope: if I held on to his string of light long enough, I would eventually come out on the other side.

But in the meantime, my thoughts relentlessly blasted out on repeat, *"I LOVED her with all my heart, giving the relationship EVERYTHING, and STILL wasn't good enough for her and her family! I'm not good enough—I'm NOT good enough! I don't have value! I've worked, and I've worked, and I'm STILL STRUGGLING! Maybe her family was right—I'll never amount to anything! Maybe I AM a LOSER! I don't have value. I AM A LOSER! No one likes me! I DON'T LIKE ME!!!"*

As the torment persisted, a realization that even "losers" needed to make a living hit; my hours were cut at the extras casting office as the economic recession was in full swing!

I'd get a job, but then I'd quit that job. I'd get another job, then quit that! I'd break down in the middle of a shift and start crying while delivering corporate lunch orders, quit on the spot, and go home. This happened every time the darkness went full force, rendering me helpless. The days of semi-depression were a blessing compared to the extremely dark and emotionally uncontrollable moments that would overtake me.

Most of my days were spent in bed, which served as my refuge and hiding place away from the darkness and pain. I grew weary of fighting what had become a losing battle. Reaching a breaking point while growing tired of not receiving a resolution from God, a decision was made to stop resisting the darkness.

I got a job as a bar back at a Middle Eastern dive bar in Glendale where people were upbeat, a little naughty, and fun to be around. It was a community of semi-drunken *bros* and *broettes*. Although yours truly wasn't a drinker, he still had fun mixing it up with the intoxicated crowds of lost and broken people: they carried their version of that darkness, which was comforting to be around. These fun-chasing people were superficially entertaining; *meaningful relationships? Get outta here with that nonsense!*

Drugs were never in the picture for me (à la Aunt Sona's dire warning), but occasionally downing a beer or two, along with a shot of vodka, with some of our bar patrons who'd insist on treating me, would be a thing. Of course, there would be instant regret because of my extremely low tolerance for alcohol.

MY WORLD WAS SHATTERED

"Love" was a lie—an enemy. The thought of marriage grossed me out and made me want to vomit! *How could anyone trust to give themselves over to a stranger only to be crushed in this way!?*

"Get married, have kids, and build a life together." I laughed in endless pain at the concept, and so a vow was made never to partake in any of those things.

Thus, a flirtatious party boy was born as he dated casually left and right, living strictly for his self-enjoyment—the alternative was not worth the gamble: being played and crushed by people. Never again would I give myself over to anyone! NEVER! That version of *"Nick"*... was **DEAD.**

Mom always did her best to reassure that things would eventually be okay, but it was no use: one minute, frailty would overtake me, and the next, I'd aggressively switch off the radio after hearing a song that reminded me of my ex. The darkness had consumed me— it was my partner in crime, having become a permanent part of my persona—everyone else was a potential enemy. The darkness validated my feelings, never trying to brush aside my deep hurt, like most people.

However, not all was lost. God was still there, protecting, healing, and honing my *Superpower* beyond comprehension, as it lay dormant. What the darkness was fueling for destruction, God would eventually transform into an invaluable creative asset.

A new path would soon be forged ... that of light. But first ... it was time for this now prodigal son to run crying back home to his momma and papa.

ELEVEN

OUT OF
THE ASHES

Every restaurant and establishment in town had about 100–300 applicants during the economic recession! Finding work in LA became a nightmare, and the extras casting office slashed hours drastically, even more so. Hopes of working in film and voice-over were also nonexistent: some small gigs were booked here and there, but nothing groundbreaking.

It had been four years since my move to LA, and I had nothing to show for it. My energy was split when it came to committing to one career path, and the most that was accomplished in production was assistant-type work. Plus, the lack of confidence made it hard to pursue anything worthwhile.

I just needed a part-time job until I could figure out my next move, but doors weren't opening; instead, they were being slammed in my face!

"I'm applying all over, but everyone is giving me the runaround!" I vented passionately to Mom over the phone. She remained silent ... then, offered, "Come home."

Moving back in with my family wasn't how I pictured my late 20s to be, nor was being a "loser," but here we were folks! It wasn't living with them that was the issue; it was knowing that I couldn't "make it" on my own!

Life seemed to have conspired against me, and my go-getter days were long gone! But regardless, there was still some fight left in me, and as depression transformed into anger, the drive to succeed kicked in!

GET A JOB MAN!

$2,300.00 was all that was left to my name, and it would only be a matter of time before that was gone! Did Mom tell me not to worry about buying food and to eat whatever she cooked? Of course, she did. And did I insult her by refusing until I could make my own money and contribute to the household? Of course I did!

While complaining to Janet on our living room couch, she got an inspired idea and suggested, "You know ... there's a new Apple Store here in town. Why don't you go and apply there?" Apple products were a childhood favorite of mine, and at that moment, a tiny glimmer of hope was birthed.

When Janet mentioned food stamps, my cringe factor kicked into overdrive, but hey ... if "mooching" off Mom wasn't going to be a survival option ... it was time to hit rock bottom and ask the government for a handout!

Sitting in my *beat-up* Toyota Corolla, I stared down the welfare building from the parking lot—talk about feeling like absolute trash!

Once inside, the social worker kindly explained my monthly EBT food allotment—$250.00. Defenses went through the roof when she brought up EBT cash— "NO, please! I'm going to find a job and make my own money! The EBT food stamps are enough!" The social worker paused and looked at me like I was from outer space. She then smiled, happily shook my hand, and wished me a "Good luck with everything, Nick."

The "good luck" paid off—I landed a job at the Apple Store! It provided me with a steady stream of income in an environment that encouraged social interaction—win/win!

Answering product questions wasn't my only role; customers would confidingly open up about their personal lives, and to my shock, helpful advice would effortlessly flow right out of me—*what was I, some kind of counselor now?*

After coming home from work, I'd plop onto my bed and wonder if things would ever be ok again; the darkness had somewhat dissipated, but in its place was this uncertain haze that lingered: figuring out how to get back to *me,* was confusing—like trying to solve a huge mental labyrinth.

Now, fortunately, my family knew exactly what was needed: a surprise 30th Birthday party! After all, it's what every man who feels like a failure needs!

"SURPRISE!"

Coming home after a long day at work, semi-depressed, I had about 40 relatives screaming in delight! Balloons were taped to the wall, under an adorable homemade "30th Birthday" sign. And what good is a birthday party without streamers? There were tons of them hanging from the ceiling! *Let's see ... thirty,* single, and still didn't have my life together. To top it off ... a celebration?

What my family planned was genuinely touching, so instead of deciding to dig myself into a hole and die immediately, a brave, happy face was put on, and everyone was thanked for coming. Admittedly, it was a great party though!

When you're on the fence of uncertainty during
the rebuilding phase of your life, it isn't easy.
Deep down, there was something that I wanted
to do more than anything else in the world.
I just needed the right push to realize it fully.
That's when God stepped in.

Mom silently lingered in my bedroom doorway watching me lying flat on my bed, staring at the ceiling. I knew she was there, but I didn't feel like talking—there were more important things to focus on, like self-pity. She stood there for what felt like forever, then out of the blue, she softly relayed a message that didn't even seem like it came from her: "You don't have a full-time job, a girlfriend, or her family's pressure on your shoulders anymore. You're free to do what you've always wanted to do since you were a kid ... become an actor."

A light instantaneously turned on in my mind as my eyes widened, and something lifted right off my body; a tiny flame of inspiration was ignited! That was the first time Mom had openly expressed her support of my becoming an actor! She had given her blessing while simultaneously breaking the overbearing oppression that my ex's parents had spoken over my life!

FREEDOM!

Freedom to pursue a field of interest without judgment or compromise! There was no one left to bow down to or to appease with a full-time job—no one's family to "look good for"—*to please.*

Mom's speech was infused with spirit, igniting my unapologetic passion for acting as it surged back into my body and saturated my heart with excitement! *And.... ACTION!*

BECOME AN ACTOR!

It was time to dive full force into the arts! Some money was set aside for a brand-new iMac, a studio-quality microphone, and pro audio editing software. A new voice-over demo was created, and copies were mailed to talent agencies all over the Bay Area! There was no *Plan B!* Never again would any compromising of self take place—not for anyone! Losing everything developed in me a *nothing left to lose* attitude! It was time to have one focus:

Become An Actor!

The best talent agency in the Bay Area, J.E. Talent, signed me on after hearing my C.D., and their head of V.O. at the time, DeeDee, said, "Nick, you will book!"

My first BIG voice-over role was a TV commercial spot for California Lotto as the voice of Santa's Reindeer. In the spot, Santa sits in his sleigh, stuck in modern-day traffic, while falling asleep at the reins. The animatronic reindeer looks at the camera and suggests audiences give Santa a break from delivering presents by gifting scratchers instead.

The gig was booked one day before the recording session, which meant having to join SAG (the actor's union) ASAP (since it was a union job). $2,200.00 ... that's what it cost to join SAG at the time. How much money did that savings account still have? $2,300.00.

My entire family erupted with excitement as the California Lotto spot aired; Janet quickly rushed at me with a big hug, and my (now) brother-in-law Gabriel announced, "You've arrived!" Good things were happening for once! Calls from my agents were a weekly occurrence, with nonstop audition requests, callbacks, and bookings! Mom's spirit-filled speech had reignited my passion, and a successful future was now in sight!

JEWISH MOM OFFER ALERT!

After a few short years of working in V.O. consistently, a mind-blowing offer would poke its head via my "Jewish Mom."

Let me explain this one...

"Jewish Mom," a.k.a. "J.M."

Marsha Goodman (her real name) was Vice President of Casting and voice directing at DIC Entertainment and had voice-directed everything from *The Real Ghost Busters* to *Inspector Gadget: Her Superpower—lovingly putting you in your place!*

Back in the day, Marsha discovered my ability to morph into various characters at one of her workshops in LA, called me a nut, handed me her business card, and told me to stay in touch. She would eventually come to dub herself my "Jewish Mom" and help me book several animated projects. The woman was and is a sweetheart serving a healthy dose of tough love.

In true "Jewish Mom" fashion, Marsha sent my new voice demo to her friend's voice-over agency in Beverly Hills, who had expressed interest in representing me—but—I'd have to move back to LA.

Although it was one of the world's most powerful voice-over agencies, there was hesitation to move back. My experiences in LA were not that great—reliving the past didn't sound appealing.

After talking it over with Mom, she gave me her blessing, urging that I should at least try it out since acting would be my only focus, with only myself to answer to. Plus, if things didn't work out, I could always move back—no biggie!

So I took Marsha up on her talent agency referral offer, and my request to be transferred to the LA Apple Store was approved! Three years after living in Northern California, it was time to head back ... to the jungle!

TWELVE

BACK TO THE JUNGLE

My spot was a one-car garage that was fully converted into a studio apartment and attached to a house that was owned by a sweetheart of an Armenian woman named Emma. Or, as I like to call her, **"Emma Tantig"** (Auntie Emma in Armenian)—*Her Superpower: healing your soul with homemade delicacies.* She was a distant in-law that Aunt Sona hooked me up with after I expressed my desperate need for a cheap place.

Emma wasn't just a landlord; she was like a second mom. The rent was an easy $550.00 a month, with all utilities included! Her intention toward me was to be as supportive as possible in my pursuit of acting, which made her a Godsend. By the way, Emma was a spectacular cook who would knock from the other side of my wall, signaling me to go into her house for Armenian coffee, breakfast, lunch, or dinner. What delectable delights Emma had prepared would have been anybody's guess, but you knew it would be amazing!

So, with rent being dirt cheap via a saint for a landlord and four short working days at Apple, the runway to my acting career was clear ... and I ... was ready for take-off!

My daily schedule:

Commute to the Beverly Hills V.O. agency for about an hour and a half in gridlocked traffic. After finishing a round of V.O. auditions, hop back into the Toyota Corolla and zip back to my place in the valley through traffic for about another hour. Get home, quickly prepare and scarf down lunch,

take a breather, head to the gym in traffic, and blast through workouts. Head back to my place for a quick shower, commute to my part-time job at the Apple Store, help close and clean up, and commute back to my place by 11:00 pm, collapse onto my bed ... and do it all again the next day!

As if my schedule wasn't insane enough, theatrical representation in the world of on-camera acting incrementally piqued my interest—*why not?*

After reaching out to my good friend Melanie (former co-worker and pal from my days at the extras casting office), she set me up with an *auntie-like* talent manager, and about six months later, I booked the role of Aleek Al Moosari on the new NBC political drama *State of Affairs,* starring Katherine Heigl and Alfre Woodard!

This was big! My family cheered and celebrated alongside me, and there was something so rewarding about unapologetically pursuing what my creative impulses had been calling me to do!

The role of Al Moosari took about a week to complete, and after returning to my trailer to wrap up the day, the talent manager called, screaming, "Hi, honey! They all LOVED you! They loved what you did so much that they want you to recur for a few more episodes!

Although my character was set up as a one episode Middle Eastern villain, I played him as a cool, laid-back all-American dude. This prompted production to have me ditch the Middle Eastern accent, making for one loveably disturbed performance. Al Moosari ended up recurring for four episodes on *State of Affairs!*

Life was flowing, and a character initially slated for one episode became a smash hit with producers and audiences alike!

Customers at the Apple Store recognized me from the show, and some even waited to take a picture during my 15 minute break—it was all very surreal!

While helping a married couple purchase an iPhone, the husband nudged his wife multiple times, signaling in my direction with his head. She told him to stop it, so he dropped the subtlety and asked, "Okay, are you on that TV show *State of Affairs?*" In response to his inquiry, I relayed a "Yes...," causing him and his wife to erupt into sudden excitement; the guy fanboyed like crazy: "Man, I love your character! Even though he's a terrorist, I'd grab beers with him—*he's cool!*"

My life had transformed creatively! And as a side note, so did my Toyota Corolla—she was dying out on me! My cousin John (who worked in auto repair and resale) asked, "What kind of car are you looking for?" "Nothing luxury, just something to get me around," I pleaded. John stressed, "Okay, but what kind of cars do you like?"

My passion for Jeeps surfaced—"Well, one day, I'd like to be driving a black Jeep." John then texted me a picture of a black Jeep! He asked, "Like this one?"—Double Take! John added, "This just came in last week. Do you want it?"

After letting him know I wasn't in the market for something costly, John generously hooked me up with a FAT family discount, and that Jeep was mine!

Shortly after, while shooting an episode of *State of Affairs,* art began imitating life: while on a heist, my character Al Moosari switches from a Toyota Corolla to a Jeep! *Cam'an, that's unbelievable!*

After wrapping *State of Affairs,* a flood of auditions came through from my manager and agent, including a booking for the lead in an Iranian film, *MADARAN (MOTHERS),* which became Oscar-qualified! Life got super crazy, super fast! Almost every casting office in town wanted to see me. However, as time passed, the relentless nature of the hustle began to exhaust and eat away at me. My life's sole purpose was defined by the need to book high-quality roles that left an impact, which was problematic: most of the opportunities presented to me would eventually be for menial parts with no depth or creativity.

Begrudgingly agreeing to go up for throw-away parts, just to make the talent manager and agent happy, ate away at my self-worth as an artist. The rapid forward momentum in both V.O. and on camera that was once experienced upon moving to LA, had transitioned into the all-dreaded *dry spell!*

My newfound identity of "Actor" was threatened by the lack of consistent bookings, alongside gigs that didn't gel with the quality of work I had hoped to do. My artistry was being insulted as the industry limited me to auditioning mostly for roles about my ethnicity, consisting of a few lines here and there.

Since it seemed there were no quality roles available within the context of being Middle Eastern, being left out in the cold unless it came to, *"We need someone to say a line in Arabic and then get shot"* was the norm—so dumb! Why did there need to be some nefarious reason for a Middle Eastern character to exist in a movie or TV show?

Thus, a negative mental spiral began as the stereotyping that was once endured throughout my life, was now being amplified and aggressively projected at me from the entertainment industry.

Fortunately, there were two relatives in LA with whom solace could be found: Cousin Seta (in her 70s) and Cousin Maren (in her 80s). Like I've said before ... *lots of cousins!*

When things got emotionally heavy, I'd default to a visit with either of these Women of God.

Cousin Seta Balejian owned an alteration shop in Thousand Oaks that was appropriately titled, *Seta's Alterations & Shoe Repair—Her Superpower: piercing your soul with powerful truth bombs!*

We'd share a piping hot pizza in the back area of her shop, and she'd hear an earful of my frustrated rants—offering up the same advice every time—"It's going to happen for you—something big will happen, but it's going to happen in your later years!"

Our discussion was interrupted by the dinging sound of her shop's doorbell—a customer walked in, ready to pick up her hemmed pants. Seta walked over to the front desk and got down to business, but things took an awkward turn.

After the customer stated, "Thank you! I don't know how you do it, Seta," Seta firmly raised her arm into the air, pointed her finger directly at a picture of Jesus that hung on her shop's wall, and passionately revealed without any hesitation, "It's Him, Jesus." The customer responded dismissively, "That's nice, Seta. How much do I owe you?" Seta was taken aback as she paused and stared at the customer with a look of "EXCUSE ME?" She wasn't about to let this lady slide; Seta aggressively reaffirmed, "Nooo, it's not *'NICE,'* it's **HIM** ... **JESUS!** HE'S the one who helps me!"

Experiencing instant secondhand embarrassment, I ducked thinking, *"What is she doing!? Why is she vehemently arguing with a paying customer about Jesus!!!?"* I didn't get it. Meanwhile, my head stayed down until the customer left.

When I wasn't making the trek to Seta's (and experiencing secondhand embarrassment), I'd pay a visit to **Cousin Maren Karalian—***Her Superpower: teleporting you to different worlds.* Maren was an 18-year-old stuck in an 80-year-old's body, and her lovable, childlike energy fueled her passion for life! She was tiny but housed a gigantic spirit. Maren self-published two books of poetry based on heart-wrenching true stories—she was GOOD. Maren's writing poured out from the depths of her soul—you'd melt hearing her recite the text—she even got me choked up a few times.

Life's challenges and lessons were themes that were always discussed openly with Maren; she was like a grandmother to me. Once-in-a-blue-moon visits with her turned into bi-weekly hang outs, including driving her around to grocery stores and helping her run errands. Maren was also a Woman of God, just like Seta.

My constant visits with both eventually elicited comments from Janet and Mary (my sisters): "Why are you hanging out with old ladies?" "What do you get out of being around them?" They couldn't conceive a motive, nor could I at the time.

But before we get ahead of ourselves...
CARE BEAR ... STARE!

Waltzing into my studio apartment after another hard day's work, I was BEAT: my eyes were droopy, and my mind was numb—it was time to go to bed. Just then, an email came through from Marsha Goodman with the subject line: "Care Bears Animated Series." My eyes instantly lit up! "WHAT!? *CARE BEARS!?* I LOVED *Care Bears!*"

It was the opportunity of a lifetime—to read for the new animated series *Care Bears: Unlock The Magic!*

GRUMPY BEAR & TENDERHEART BEAR

Of all the characters, they stood out as my childhood favorites! Energy overtook me as I hopped into my makeshift V.O. booth (that Dad helped me build). *Care Bears* was right up my alley! The illustrations had major appeal, the script was superb, and the storyline of combating evil with *caring* ... was touching.

About three weeks after submitting my audition, Marsha crowned me as the official voice of Grumpy and Tenderheart! My prayers were answered, and the next nine months would be spent recording numerous episodes for *Care Bears: Unlock The Magic!*

Care Bears represented the pinnacle of voice acting! The gig meant everything to me: two leads in an animated series—that didn't happen every day! This was it—the project that would eradicate the remnants of that inner turmoil from years past, replacing it with fulfillment and a sense of achievement!

Hold your horses there partner ...

A few months into recording the series, that inner void was still intact, and it continued to grow exponentially.

While left unsettled, I realized that achieving a major career goal wouldn't be enough to heal all the past trauma that had blindsided me over many years. Life became painful upon discovering that even a successful acting career wasn't going to do it for me.

And if landing the job of my dreams wasn't going to be enough … then what would be?

THIRTEEN

IT'S JUST "ZA-BEE-DEE" HONEY

had been flirting with the idea of moving back up north in 2018, but I'd do it after wrapping up *Care Bears*. Living in LA was not mentally sustainable, having exacerbated my feelings of isolation and stress—I was lacking in community. Plus, opportunities for meaningful work had dried up in the on-camera world, so what was the point in staying? I hadn't exactly been running into the most genuine people either (can you say, *covert narcissists?*). Boy, was LA packed with them! It seemed as if people were programmed to use you and toss you aside when they couldn't, so it was time to take my wins and leave the jungle!

One day while refueling my Jeep, a call came through from the talent manager. Rolling my eyes immediately, waiting to hear what bit-player role she had in store for me, I took the call as she excitedly relayed, "Hi, honey! I got you an audition for a television series called *The Chosen.*" The title borderline gave me chills as she went on to say, "You're auditioning for the role of Shmuel, and he's a series regular!"

The writing was superb, and I was off-book that same night. Memorizing lines had posed a challenge with scripts in the past, as most lacked in every aspect of creativity, spirit, and heart. However, this thing was jam-packed: the setting was highly vivid, with three-dimensional characters. I couldn't believe it was a project about Jesus' ministry.

The last thing I wanted to do was audition for a faith-based project, but the script had me hooked! After sending off my self-tape for

Shmuel, a shower needed to be taken; what an insufferable human being—*yuck!*

Just days later, the talent manager called screaming, "Hi, honey! You have a call back for *The Chosen!* They want you to go in person to read for Dallas Jenkins, the director, but it's for a different character." My manager tried her best to pronounce the name of this new character: "It's for ... the role of em ... let's see ... Zeb, Zib ... eh ... Zeb ..." She then decided to throw in the towel and settle on, "It's just 'ZA-BEE-DEE' honey ... it's just 'ZA-BEE-DEE.'"

"ZA-BEE-DEE???"

What in blazes was a "Zabeedee?" It was the strangest name ever heard! After trying to get more info out of my manager, she cut me off—"I'm sending you the audition sides now, okay honey?" *(Me: "But, but...")* "Okay, sweetie"—click.

After printing the sides, I saw that this guy "Zabeedee" was a dad—father of James and John to be exact. My mind skipped at the word *"father."* First of all, I didn't look old enough to play a dad, nor did I desire to be anyone's daddy—*why was I being requested to read for this part?*

Then, I noticed his age—**MID-50s**. My brain EXPLODED! *"Did I just read what I think I just read!?"* Looking back at the character description, it turned out that I wasn't going bonkers. "50s!? 50s!!!??? **FIFTIES!!!!????** They want me to read for a guy in his **FIFTIES!!!???"**

Were these people on crack!?

Why in the world would anyone think that a guy in his mid-30s could pull off playing a 50-year-old fisherman unless they *were* ... on *CRACK!?* After months of a major dry spell, I was stuck with "ZA-BEE-DEE"—GREAT!

At least the script was good, and the imagery of Zebedee that was evoked felt like a direct download from God: he exuded a part of Dad's rough persona, with a whole serving of Mom's heart. His costuming and outlook on life were all there, ripe and ready for the picking! Having memorized all nine pages, it was time to meet with Dallas.

While seated in the lobby of the casting office, something strange happened; he was gone! "Za-bee-dee" had left the building! My creative inclination came to a sudden halt, refusing to perform—mind, body, and soul gave out at that moment, exhausted after years of auditioning.

Just then, Beverly Holloway, the casting director, stepped out of the audition room and called, *"Nick?"* No longer feeling like I had a horse in the race, I loosened up, raised an eyebrow, and replied with a playful, *"Beverly...?"* To which she laughed.

While letting myself into the audition room, a tall giant with a husky voice charged at me like a big kid—"Hi, I'm Dallas. Thanks for coming in." My response was, "Sup Bruh!?" He and Beverly chuckled as I made myself comfortable on the audition chair. There were two scenes to perform: one occurred inside "The Hammer" (pub), and the other was "The Miraculous Catch of the Fish."

Because my attitude was one of carelessness, interacting with the reader was direct—I spat out my lines like a *know-it-all jerk*.

Poking fun at Dallas in between scenes also took hold—there was something about him that made me want to be ultra-sarcastic and humorous. Connecting with Dallas was more of a priority than the project itself, as I took to the guy instantly. He would ask, "Are you familiar with the story of what happens after Jesus calls James and John?" Having zero interest in the subject matter, my deadpan response was, "Yeah, he takes them out for burrito bowls at Chipotle." Thrown by my remark, Dallas chuckled as Beverly giggled alongside him and commented, "That's just great." She scribbled something on her notepad and thanked me for coming in.

While on my way to work, the talent manager called screaming, "YOU BOOKED IT, HONEY! HAHAHA! YOU BOOKED *THE CHOSEN!*"

It had been about a month and a half since the audition, and her excitement made zero sense. She stressed, *"The Chosen,* honey! They want you for 'Za-bee-dee!'" I instantly thought, *"There's no way these people took my audition seriously! 50-year-old fisherman!!? C'MON! Were these people nuts!? Or—on CRACK!?"*

Ding! An email from the talent manager...

While I was having breakfast with Auntie Emma (my landlord) the following day, my talent manager asked if she could say *"yes"* to *The Chosen* on my behalf. Her email read something like, "Hi, Honey! I just wanted to confirm that you're good to go for *The Chosen.* It would be for two weeks of filming in Texas. Let me know, sweetie!"

Rage took control of my entire body! So much so that it had Auntie Emma do a double take. "Za-bee-dee" was *the* final slap in the face after years of enduring many slaps within an industry that was off its rocker, and I was DONE!

Chatter broke out in my mind, screaming—

"I'M SO SICK OF ALL THIS!"
"THESE INDUSTRY PEOPLE CAN KICK ROCKS!"
"YOU'RE NOT EVEN BEING OFFERED A LEAD!"
"YOU DON'T NEED THIS CRAP IN YOUR LIFE!"
"PEOPLE AREN'T VALUING YOU!"
"THIS ISN'T AGE-APPROPRIATE!"
"ENOUGH IS ENOUGH!"
"DON'T LET THEM USE YOU!"

My blood boiled over! After deciding to put my foot down, and stand up for myself, an aggressively typed-out email response of "NO!" was sent to my talent manager. Concerned about my tone, she reached out via phone and softly asked, "Hi honey ... is everything okay?"

We had a quick chat about my frustrations with the entertainment industry, and then the call ended.

I had a great thing going with *Care Bears* and a secure job at the Apple Store, so why risk both for some supporting role set to appear in a single web series episode? NO THANK YOU!

The onslaught of chatter grew rapidly, orbiting my head, screaming even louder—

"THIS IS SUCH A STUPID PROJECT!"
"DON'T DO IT!"
"IF THEY WANT YOU THAT BAD, THEY SHOULD PAY YOU A YEAR'S WORTH OF LIVING EXPENSES!"
"YOU'RE GOING TO GET FIRED FROM YOUR GIGS!"

Ding! Another email from the talent manager...

"Hi honey, the casting director said that production would love to work with you." My response to that: **"NO! NO! NO!"** The talent manager replied, "Okay, honey, I'll let them know." My internal response: *"Yeah, you do that! You let them know! 50-year-old fisherman,* *my butt!"* Auntie Emma was captivated by the intense tennis match as she gently popped another olive into her mouth.

Ding! Then another email...

It was the talent manager ... again! She wrote, "Hi honey, they said they'd be willing to work with your schedule." Turning to Emma, my eyes rolled like two heavy bowling balls. *"Why are they trying to accommodate me? Did no one else want to do this role? This must be one joke of an operation for them to be THAT desperate. Why did they want me?! NO ONE wants me!"*

While drowning in an emotional heat storm, a tiny burst of inspiration was able to pierce through and reach my heart. I emailed my manager: "Okay, I'll do it ONLY if the Apple Store AND *Care Bears* give me two weeks off. I'll let you know by tonight. Thank you." The talent manager responded with (you guessed it), "Okay honey."

SELF-SABOTAGE TIME!

It was now time to request two weeks off from both jobs: *Care Bears* & Apple. The good news was that *The Chosen* needed me from late November to early December, meaning it would be nearly impossible to take time away from the retail job and *Care Bears*. Too much would need to be shifted to accommodate such a crazy request. I had it in the bag: request time off, get shot down, and inevitably say "No," to *The Chosen*.

First up was Marsha Goodman. After exiting the V.O. booth, I walked over to Marsha, and egged her on: "Hey J.M. (Jewish Mom), there's this *JESUS* project that wants to book me for two weeks, but I'd have to fly to Texas to do it—you know what, I'll just let them know I can't do it."

Marsha went quiet with a sudden blank expression that overtook her face. She stared off into the ether transfixed, abruptly snapped out of it, turned to me, and casually recommended,

"It sounds like a good opportunity, you should do it."

What...!?

My urgent plea: "But ... we have *Care Bears* to record!" Marsha went silent, drew another blank, snapped out of it, and reassured, "You can just make it up when you come back." My jaw fell to the floor. This wasn't going according to plan, so things had to get personal—another pushback: "But J.M., it's a show about **JESUS!**" Growing weary of my whining, Marsha was so over me: "OKAY!? So go and do it!"

What a disappointment—talk about a huge letdown! But not all was lost. My shift at Apple was coming up within a few hours, and getting shot down by my boss would be my saving grace!

While I was on the busy sales floor, the scheduling manager darted by, heading toward his office. Rushing after him, I squeezed through as his office door closed. After asking him for time off to shoot *The Chosen*, the all too obvious, "I'm sorry, Nick, we can't accommodate that during the holidays" would surely follow. Instead, something odd happened: he stared off into the ether like Marsha, drew a blank, suddenly snapped out of it, looked at me, and urgently recommended, "You should do it. It sounds like a great opportunity."

Oh C'mon...!

My jaw fell to the floor—*again*. Seriously, was *EVERYONE* on *crack!?* Rebutting, "But what about my shifts?" would surely sabotage his decision. He paused, contemplated, then turned to me and kindly offered, "Oh that's okay, we'll just take you off the schedule." My jaw went from being on the floor to crashing right through it! It turned out that everyone *WAS* on *CRACK!*

Staying true to my word, an email was begrudgingly sent to my talent manager, saying, "Yes" to *The Chosen!*

YEE-HAW!

After touching down at Dallas Fort Worth International Airport, my jadedness slowly dissipated after being greeted by **Shelly**, our shuttle driver—*Her Superpower: prophesying over your life*. While overlooking a sea of parked cars, I spotted a beautiful lady flashing a gigantic smile and waving joyously in my direction. She seemed to have a strange glow around her: **Shelly Smith**—a Woman of God. She would quickly come to be known as everyone's "Cool Aunt" on the set of *The Chosen* and, for some (including myself), a dear friend.

No more "Mr. Nice Guy." If I was going to be forced back into on-camera acting, then *unapologetic freedom* would be my top priority. My on-set shenanigans consisted of doing character voices in between takes to acting out in sarcasm when given direction by Dallas: while demonstrating how to safely step into Zebedee's boat, my jabber began to distract him, and Dallas rightfully snapped at me, "Nick, can you pay attention? I'm trying to show you how to get in the boat safely."

I responded, "Oh, thank you so much for showing us how to get on a boat! I would have never known otherwise!" Proceeding to jump into the boat, I paced around effortlessly and facetiously announced, "Wow, it's a good thing you showed us how to do this!"

The other actors immediately placed their hands over their mouths in shock, but I didn't care. What's the worst that could have happened? Getting fired? *Bring it on!* After all ... *entertainment business?* Eh! I'd been too hurt by the ego-driven culture of it all to care anymore.

However, there was one thing left unaccounted for during my sarcastic tirade—Dallas' love language: SARCASM. *Gosh darn it!* My plan to annoy him as much as possible had backfired, as he seemingly got a kick out of my antics on some level, and I began to enjoy the company around me.

"ZEB-A-DEE"

So that's how it was pronounced! It wasn't "Za-BEE-dee" after all! Dallas was quick to correct after hearing me butcher the name. Now that I had Za-bee-dee—*I mean* Zebedee's name down, it was time to look like him!

After asking the hair and makeup team if they planned on aging me for the role, they responded, "We weren't given any notes on that." I snapped back desperately, "What!? Come on, I don't look old enough to be these guys' (Shayan & George's) dad!" It was time to take matters into my own hands!

"AGE ME!"

The hair and makeup team aged my skin, alongside coloring my hair and beard—they made me into a legit 50-year-old fisherman— it took some time though. After arriving 40 minutes late to set, Dallas asked, "Why did you take so long? We've been waiting for you." I stood my ground and confessed, "I had the hair and makeup team age me—COME ON, MAN! I don't look old enough to be their dad!" Dallas leaned in, inspected my face, and, in confusion, asked, "I don't get it ... what did they do?" Instantly insulted, I turned my head and walked away.

You know when you have that one kid in the family who's always causing a stir, but everyone loves him anyway? That was me on the set of *The Chosen*. Maybe being a part of this project wasn't going to be so bad after all. Deciding to lighten up, and have some fun ... I made peace with being a part of *The Chosen*.

FOURTEEN

STAY

The heaviness that was drowning me in LA seemed to dissipate as we shot "The Miraculous Catch of the Fish" scene during the freezing month of November. Our feet turned purple from running around in the ice-cold water, but the camaraderie on set made it all worthwhile.

George (John), Shayan (James #1), and I (Zebedee) decided to head to a popular steak house and unwind after a long day's work; we were ready to devour some well-seasoned meat, I tell ya, Texan style! Shortly after putting in our orders with the server, an unexpected call came through from my brother-in-law (Archangel) Gabriel (The Messenger). My stomach sank immediately, knowing that he wasn't one to make casual calls to my cell phone.

After excusing myself from the table, I headed into a small hallway leading up to the restrooms. I raised the phone to my ear, only to hear Gabriel urgently spit out, "Hey Nick, your mom has been telling everyone not to call you, but I thought you should know that we're here at the hospital—your dad just had a heart attack."

My stomach instantly turned as Gabriel kept the intense news coming rapid-fire style; "They're going to take him into surgery tomorrow at 9:00 a.m., and the doctor said the initial attack was a *'widow maker'*—he should have already been a goner!"

WHAT A SICK NIGHTMARE!

Dad got on the call and reassured, "Don't worry, everything will be okay. Good luck." I was at a loss for words—Dad was about to have open heart surgery and he was the one wishing ME luck! There was so much to say, but the moment rendered me helpless. The only thing I could muster up was, "Okay, Dad... I love you."

The call ended as the clanking sounds of silverware and restaurant patrons slowly drew me back into the present moment. Quietly rejoining George and Shayan at the table, my heart filled with angst. The guys looked on as I sat silently, staring at what was now a cold plate of baby back ribs. George leaned in and hesitantly asked, "Is everything okay, mate?" How to even answer that question...?

With my voice trapped at the bottom of my throat, it struggled to make its way out and break the news. The guys expressed how sorry they were and wondered what I was going to do. After a quick moment of contemplation ... a decision was made: "I have to leave the show and catch a flight back to California tonight."

"LEAVE!"

While pacing like a madman in my hotel room, the time was 11:00 p.m., and the table lamp was the only light source as I scrolled through last-minute flights on my phone. Almost immediately, the screeching voices from weeks prior, came back in full force as they amplified, teased, and screamed—

"WHY DID YOU COME HERE!?"
"YOU SHOULD HAVE NEVER DONE THIS JOB!"
"YOU'RE A TERRIBLE SON IF YOU DON'T LEAVE TO BE WITH YOUR FAMILY!"
"THEY NEED YOU!"
"YOUR DAD IS GOING TO DIE AND YOU'RE NEVER GOING TO SEE HIM AGAIN!"
"LEAVE!" "RIGHT NOW!"
"FIND A FLIGHT AND LEAVE!"
"NOW!"

My mind was held hostage, trapped in a spiritual headlock—there was no breaking free of my own accord! The guilt of being away from my family was unbearably agonizing!

STAY or LEAVE—my family needed me! STAY or LEAVE—Nick the problem solver! STAY or LEAVE—they always relied on me! STAY or LEAVE—who would be there for them!?

Unable to fight off the voices, and desperate for help, I turned to **Someone** in a high place whose very existence I had denied weeks prior, when claiming, "You probably don't even exist." This was blurted out after years of non-stop treachery that led to being disappointed in a God that had allowed it all to happen in the first place.

With no one left to turn to, I sheepishly called out, "God…? What do YOU think I should do!?" Then, to my surprise, a resoundingly deep, Fatherly voice emerged, offering a simple piece of advice…

"STAY"

The screeching voices immediately vanished the second He spoke, and the atmosphere was deafly still; my hotel room was engulfed in a protective shield of love—His voice was audibly shocking; His presence could almost be sensed.

Taken aback by His advice, I cautiously leaned into the moment and questioned, "Stay?" His response... "Stay." *Why on earth would I stay? Staying would be foolish! This was my family! My Dad! Stay!?* **STAY!?**

After attempting to push back at His directive, He caught me off guard by warning, "If you leave, you will ruin both tomorrow's shoot and your dad's chances of living."

In just a few hours, our associate producer Justen Overlander would be picking me up at 5:00 a.m. to finish shooting "The Miraculous Catch of the Fish," and time was running out—a choice had to be made!

My Dad... MY Dad. I couldn't just let him go! My Dad. He was "MY"—oh ... then, a sudden awareness ... Dad wasn't mine ... he was HIS.

Something clicked ... a deep understanding of God's love ... a kind of love that wasn't based on threats or ultimatums. He was giving me the option of heeding or ignoring His pressure-free Fatherly advice. God loved me. He loved me ... even when I had challenged His very existence. He loved me enough to let me make my own decision. *Stay* or *Leave*—the decision would ultimately be mine. God had honored His gift of *free will* ... and at that moment ... I knew that I needed to honor Him ... even if that meant never seeing Dad again.

It was about midnight when I picked up my phone and gave Mom a call: "Hi, Mom ... I've decided to stay. I feel like God wants me to." We said goodnight to each other and the call ended.

Bursting into regret-filled tears, I realized that a sacrifice had been made—my earthly father for my Heavenly one. When push came to shove, it was God as my first choice, over my own Dad! *How could that possibly have been after years of doubting if He even existed!? What was I thinking!?*

My hotel room rant-

"God! I don't know why you brought me all the way here, but I know it has to be for a reason ... and if Thanksgiving was the last time I was supposed to see my dad, then I accept that! I now know that he ultimately belongs to You! He's not mine, he's YOURS! And if you decide that you're going to take him tomorrow morning ... then I accept that!"

Fully letting go of Dad, and immediately falling onto my bed, he was released to God that night.

Soon enough, 5:00 a.m. rolled around and I found myself collapsing into Justen Overlander's arms after being greeted in the hotel lobby. He told the producers about my family's situation, and they let me know they'd been praying for my dad; I'd never been on a set where people confidently and unapologetically expressed their belief in God, let alone offered up prayers for a stranger.

That day felt like a fever dream, sending my sons off to follow Jesus joyously, while Dad was having open heart surgery in California. Saying I intensely clung to God and Jesus while being broken, out of my mind, and in a state of desperation, would have been an understatement. And oddly enough, it would be this very state of brokenness that would unforeseeably seal Zebedee's fate with *The Chosen*.

In between takes, George (John) would gleefully lean in to say, "Mate, you've got this crazy glint in your eyes!"

Moments later, Dallas called a wrap on the scene and was ready to move on to the next shot without getting Zebedee's coverage.

George and Shayan were utterly dumbfounded by the decision and made it their mission to ensure that the "crazy glint" was captured!

Frantically rushing to Dallas, George, and Shayan hopped up and down, yelling,

"You have to get Nick's coverage! Something is happening in his eyes!!!" Confused by their relentless antics, Dallas argued, "We don't need his coverage. Zebedee is finished after this episode." But my make-believe sons would not take *no* for an answer! Their unyielding tenacity convinced Dallas to begrudgingly capture one take of what the viewers of the show would end up knowing as, "Zebedee's Laugh."

It was a wrap!

Immediately walking away from the set, I called Mom for an update on Dad's surgery while everyone else was gathered around "video village," watching the playback of my performance.

Not a split second after taking my call, Mom urgently relayed, "The surgery was a success—the doctor said he will have a full recovery!"

A sudden weight was lifted off of me—I broke down into tears of joy! Dad was going to be okay! God had kept his promise!

As a part of our original deal, The Chosen agreed to fly me back to California to catch up on Care Bears records during my three days off. Those three days were used to visit Dad.

While standing in the recovery room, it was surreal seeing Dad in a hospital bed: he was still a bit high from all the meds and looked like a lost child—I'd never seen him that way.

Dad stared on for a brief moment and softly asked, "How did the shoot go?" While holding back my tears ... "Good Dad, good. I fly back in three days to finish up." Dad responded with his always encouraging, "Good ... good luck."

Our tender moment was quickly overtaken by the entrance of the *always* fantastic "Dr. Black Doogie Houser" (a term I've coined for Dad's brilliant heart surgeon). He walked confidently, radiating that "strange light" I had seen on our transport driver, Shelly Smith—by the way ... the guy looked like he was in his 20s!

Noticing my confused stare, Doc read my mind and clarified, "I'm actually 50. Don't worry, I get it all the time"—he flashed his thousand-watt smile, took out his driver's license, and held it up—"See...?" After inspecting his I.D. I took one look at him, and verbally acknowledged, "Wow, it really doesn't crack!" Doc burst out into (perfect) laughter, turned to Dad, pointed at me, and confirmed, "So *this* is the actor?"

Doc casually admitted, "You know, in all my years of performing surgery, this was the first time that we didn't use a defibrillator to jump-start a heart. All of his vitals kicked in on their own the second we put his heart back in. I've never seen anything like it in my entire career." Doc looked me dead in the eye, pointed right at Dad ... and as if relaying a message from a certain **Someone**, he stressed, "You know this was a miracle, right?"

Everything had seemingly fallen into place ... but I was left haunted. While staring at Dad in transfixed silence ... a single word echoed in my mind...

"Stay."

FIFTEEN

SHIFTING

It was back to the grind in Los Angeles, hustling through endless rounds of meaningless auditions while working my part-time job at Apple. On the retail side of things, people were getting meaner and pushier, and when it came to the entertainment business, I was getting tired of dealing with all the *actor types* and the fickle industry as a whole. I'd find myself having surprisingly scary conversations with several customers about this unshakable feeling of impending doom that was fast approaching all humanity, and they'd agree.

Escaping to Care-A-Lot with some *Care Bears* records was my go-to! Once episodes started airing, some unexpected news came in: Grumpy Bear was a fan favorite, which meant traveling to New York to interview on the *SYFY Wire* stage at *Comic-Con 2019!*

It was overwhelming, with thousands of people in costume and endless rows of colorfully decorated booths!

The night before *Comic-Con*, I bum-rushed to see everything around Manhattan, scarfed down a few slices of NY pizza, grabbed a cheesecake at *Junior's*, and rushed through *Times Square*. New York was a place I vibed with right away! People were *real*—they'd get up in my face, and I'd give it right back, receiving a laugh afterward. It was like being in Beirut all over again—*"Ahh, they're just like my family!"* The New York / *Comic-Con* trip made me appreciate how far I'd come and the people who had my back along the way!

Months after my return to Los Angeles, "Corona" was being talked about left and right.

Customers at my job would constantly express their concerns about this thing called "Corona," and because my head was stuck in the sand, it would confuse the daylights out of me. As I drove up north for what would be my surprise birthday party (yes, another one), a nationwide pandemic would be declared.

SURPRISE!

About 30 guests stood cheering in my sister Janet's backyard. She and Mary had been planning for the big 4-O for months, and not even a pandemic could compete with their passion for theme parties!

The backyard was decked out Italiano style: tables were immaculately draped with maroon cloths and strategically topped with wine bottles, surrounded by plastic grapes! My sisters even hired a portable pizza chef who cooked the BEST Italian pizzas right from his portable stonefire oven! The icing on the cake for me was when a downpour of rain drenched the awnings under which we all took cover. Mom said, "Ah, it's raining ... that means you're going to have good luck!"

A day later, Mom and I sat in the living room watching the news—California was going into lockdown for "two weeks." Right then, that deep Fatherly voice came through saying, "Put in your 30-day notice with your landlord, and bring all your stuff up north to be with your family. California will be locked down for two to three years, not two to three weeks." Once again, the voice was calm, all-knowing, loving, and direct—this time, there wouldn't be any second-guessing on my part.

The lockdown situation was both shocking and disarming for my family: we watched people behaving ruthlessly toward one another as their massively conflicting points of view collided. We decided to hold firmly to God and placed our lives in His hands; Dad's open heart surgery had woken me up to how much in control God was in our lives. However, that viewpoint didn't sit well with certain relatives, "friends," or business colleagues. Life became discouraging and hopeless as many distanced themselves from me.

Career-wise, two significant things happened: *The Chosen* took off in viewership ... and ... I left my job at Apple.

One day, after getting out of the shower, that all-knowing Fatherly voice came through to offer, "If you leave Apple, I will amplify your finances by (x-amount)." So my two weeks' notice was placed!

Only a crazy person would quit a job that was paying them to hunker down and keep in touch via Zoom. Apple was being generous: millions of people were laid off from work, and here I was, going full commando in a dying economy.

One thing I had come to realize, was that God's logic was different than ours. My boss was super confused as she asked, "Are you sure you want to quit?" After letting her know that it was a God-led decision, she urged me to stay in touch and left the door open for my return. After thanking her for everything, goodbyes were said, and once again, I jumped ... believing God would catch me.

Season 2 of *The Chosen* had commenced, and although Zebedee would be on screen for about 30 seconds in the very last episode, Dallas revealed a major plot to enlarge his role in future seasons! The audience's response to Zebedee's laugh was so overwhelming in Season 1, that the producers decided to make him a permanent part of the show!

This was great news, but sadly, *who cared?* The world of acting began to wither away for me, as did everything else that was once near and dear to my heart. The lockdowns, along with the theme of being abandoned by those whom I considered "friends," crushed what remained of my soul.

Season 2 of *The Chosen* felt different: the show was going through its growing pains, as was I. Many new cast members were added to the mix, changing the dynamics of what was once something familiar to me.

There was a strong pull ... a pull that was taking me away from everyone and everything: my priorities seemed to shift as *The Chosen* grew in popularity. While my castmates were seemingly basking in the experience of it all ... I sat back bitterly, no longer caring about achievement or "my future." A crisis was brewing, and my path was seemingly veering off into a frighteningly unknown direction.

Relationships change, people change ...
life changes; I was changing, too. And so ...
the process of being spiritually separated,
had officially begun.

As Season 3 of *The Chosen* rolled around, my inner cry for a new life intensified with an endless search for that *something*—only to reach a dead end every time. Not knowing my true self also added to the growing turmoil; even a successful acting career could no longer mask the pain as my soul's thirst for something more significant increased exponentially.

What was the problem?

After Dad's heart surgery miracle, I started to believe in God, so why wasn't I whole? Where was the joy?

Meditation didn't work, positive thinking didn't work, and it all eventually defaulted me back to the pile of trauma that had built up and clogged my internal flow over the years— *nothing of my own will worked.* Not even an acting opportunity could provide fulfillment, which was scary. Everything was wilting away; nothing satisfied, not family, money, or public notoriety. None of it was enough!

SIXTEEN

GETTING WARMER

Impromptu comedy sketches featuring *Transformers* and *The Chosen* crossover were performed by yours truly during the run of Season 3—right on set! My internal pain was growing so intensely that reverting to what comforted me as a child (performing impressions) was the only way to keep things light and fun.

Because we happened to be in Texas, where 16-wheelers ran rampant, my childhood love of *Transformers* was naturally reignited—the crew laughed hysterically at my comedy sketch performances in between set-ups, as the actors stared on in confusion.

There were four days left before my flight back to California, and we'd be on a month-long hiatus before returning. Hanging out in my designated apartment was an option, as was visiting the set. During this time, I had been mourning the loss of Cousin Maren (the Armenian Poet who passed away from health complications) and a friend of the family, Aimee, who had taken her own life during the lockdowns. It had been a few months since Maren and Aimee had passed, but the pain of losing them was still very much there.

Maren was especially weighing heavily on my heart throughout my stay in Texas, as the thought of her being gone took its toll. Her voice could be heard vividly, telling me to stop and pray in front of the mysterious grey church down the street from my apartment. She would seemingly come through every time I'd pass by it and advise, "Just step onto the property and say a prayer. You don't have to go inside."

The church courtyard displayed a charming miniature stone labyrinth, a saint statue, and an array of floral bushes. While standing, facing the church with my hands crossed, one over the other, and head bowed, the Our Father Prayer Mom taught me as a kid came to mind. But there was a strong push not to speak.

Then … what can only be described as a dense cloud of heavenly love fell over me from the sky and engulfed the entire property!

Unable to hold in all the inner turmoil, I mourned it all: feeling lost, Cousin Maren, abandonment by supposed "friends," Aimee, the lockdowns, being misunderstood—everything. Collapsing onto my knees, I sobbed uncontrollably.

After bringing myself back to a standing position, a surprisingly mischievous sense of play washed over me. Everything felt lighter, and not a moment later, yours truly was driving off to visit the set, ready for the unexpected!

HERE COMES THE CHATTERBOX!

Chatting it up with various folks who worked behind the scenes was fun! There was a swell fellow by the name of Josh (a former college footballer), and his joyous co-worker Antonia Reed (a Spanish / Native American gal with adorably braided pigtails).

After getting to know each other, Josh and I rode around on one of the golf carts during his lunch break, then we quickly swung by Antonia, picked her up, and sped off to visit the biblical set still under construction.

Josh knocked on a grimy portable office at the entrance of the biblical town and out walked one of the construction leads with full confidence, **Seth Trenda**—*His Superpower: lighting up your life fireworks-style.*

As he and his tough men came out to greet us, a powerful, otherworldly wave of transparent brightness emanated from behind them, creating a slightly blurred effect around the outlines of their heads and shoulders. The experience was dizzying—almost blinding—*I had to do a double take!*

Seth distributed yellow hard hats and vests to Josh and Antonia. Then, after taking one look at my pink polo shirt, he smirked and handed me the pink hard hat and vest to match—*we all laughed.*

After touring the construction site, Josh, Antonia, and I thanked Seth for letting us take a peek—we handed him back the safety gear.

Seth held out his hand, as mine seemingly magnetized onto it—we shook for a slightly prolonged amount of time, as an unexplainable energetic exchange took place—it was as if we had known each other long before we had ever met.

Snapping out of it, we said our goodbyes and I eventually caught up with Josh and Antonia, who were already in the golf cart waiting for me. As we drove off, I looked back at Seth's portable office, curiously confused.

Back at base camp, Antonia and I hung out in the golf cart in front of her portable office while waiting for Josh to run an errand. We were surrounded by white gravel, which made that Texas heat all the more intense!

The one-on-one moment with Antonia allowed me to come up for air and unload my very heavy *tender ... heart* (see what I did there?).

After hearing everything she needed to hear, Antonia paused momentarily and urged, "... let's go into my office." **Antonia Reed**—*Her Superpower: seeing what others don't.*

As I stood across from Antonia, she lingered ... waiting for the words to come. Upon breaking her introspective silence, she rhetorically stated, "Do you know why you feel excluded from your castmates? It's because you're on a different path than they are." Her conviction was both disarming and confusing. *Different path?*

Antonia confessed, "I don't usually talk about this ... but when I look at people, I don't see them ... I see the light that's in and around them. And that light is either weak, strong, or nonexistent."

Sensing that she may have lost me, Antonia clarified, "When you first walked into this office to get tested, I wasn't even looking up at you; I had my head down, and the next thing I knew, this wave of light and love hit me right in the face as the door was opened. That's what made me look up—it was all emanating from you."

In response to my bewildered reaction, Antonia cut to the chase: "People are turning away from the light growing inside you because they don't understand it and aren't ready for it—it scares them."

As I tried wrapping my head around the info-overload, Antonia skipped a beat and glanced over to my left as if being interrupted by somcone who had just let themselves into the room. Diverting my attention to the door, there was no one there.

Antonia turned to me and immediately acknowledged, "You're mourning a grandmother figure." Caught off guard by her remark, the only response I could muster was a "What?" Antonia didn't flinch—she reconfirmed, "You're mourning a grandmother figure—she's short, petite, has round white hair, and she's to your left supporting you."

Off my growing paranoia, Antonia clarified, "I see passed on loved ones. It's a gift I've had since I was a little girl." The lady may have sounded nuts, but she was being very matter-of-fact about the whole thing, which ... in turn ... made her sound even MORE nuts!

With a *gotcha* comment, I attempted to discredit her claim by revealing, "My grandmother passed away during my childhood—I'm not mourning her." Antonia confidently reaffirmed, "You're mourning a grandmother figure, and that's why she's here supporting you."

It took me quite a while to realize that Antonia wasn't talking about my grandmother ... she was talking about a grandmother FIGURE!

Cousin Maren!

The same Maren who told me to pray in front of that mysterious church! She was technically my cousin, but Maren always called me her "#1 grandchild." She was like a grandmother (figure) to me!

Antonia shifted her attention to my right, held her arm up, and waved it around as she revealed, "You also have an entire team supporting you to your right—you have a lot of light and support all around you."

After cautiously sneaking a peek to my right, I turned my attention back to Antonia and sarcastically asked, "Okay, who are you? 'The Oracle' from *The Matrix?*"

Antonia chuckled, but only for a brief moment—*having just received a vision*. She then went on to relay an otherworldly message as only a *true* Oracle could: "You're going through a lot right now, and that's why you have so much support around you... Your light is growing, and it's only going to get stronger. After you come back from your month-long break, your supporters are going to give you one big push forward, and from that point on, everything will move quickly for you. You will affect everyone on set ... and you will be the one they all look to as the example." Antonia gazed at me in awe and concluded with full realization...

"You're going to be a completely different man."

SEVENTEEN

RADIOACTIVE LOVEFIRE

Back in good ol' Texas ... yes we were, I tell ya, yeehaw!!! It was time to wrap up Season 3 of *The Chosen!* Production had put me back up in my designated apartment, but the place felt different—something had changed: violent tectonic plates began rubbing up against each other deep inside me, as a sea of discomfort began to stir, and the urge to walk around the kitchen island took hold.

Something strange and brand new was about to happen—an internal eruption! Out of the blue, an image of a golden gilded cage shot over my right shoulder and projected onto the ceiling! It stopped me dead in my tracks: the image seemingly appeared out of nowhere, and it wasn't something that was imagined of my own will.

What the...?

The dome-shaped cage was immaculate, with thick golden bars and spectacularly adorned with a bouquet of shiny diamonds and red rubies draped all over the top. Its door was open, and a jaw-dropping antique-style shimmering golden key was slotted right through the keyhole—I'd never seen something so blindingly beautiful!

My attention was quickly diverted by the sudden appearance of a secondary image that shot over my left shoulder and floated opposite the gilded cage: a simple run-of-the-mill green pasture with a white dirt road leading up to the horizon; in this image, the sky was a perfect baby blue, and the sun's warmth kissed my face.

Why was I being shown this?

Turning back to the gilded cage, I heard aloud that deep, Fatherly voice reveal, *"The Chosen is at a crossroads. It will be increasing in popularity, and many will be walking into this—do you want it?"* Walking into that cage was very tempting—it would have given me unlimited finances, an abundance of success, ultimate fame, and worldwide notoriety.

Before making a hasty decision, I broke away from the cage's mesmerizing trance and walked around the kitchen island to shake the entire thing off, but it followed.

Glancing back at the gilded cage to reconsider its offer ... I suddenly noticed that it was placed on top of an elevated pedestal, surrounded by silhouettes of lively sinister crowds—they revealed disturbing Joker-like smiles as they cheerfully applauded in *the most* superficial way—*what an overly indulgent pile of crap!*

Quickly diverting my attention back to the green pasture, the air was crisp, emitting a calming clearness. Although not as exciting as the elevated cage, it felt like home—a haven of ultimate peace.

Out of sheer curiosity, I called out, "Am I supposed to pick one of these?" The Fatherly voice answered, "You will have whichever one you pick and everything that goes along with it."

All sales were final! No returns, exchanges, or refunds.

Looking back at the gilded cage, anger and disgust erupted out of my belly for its representation of phony celebrity culture, idol worship, superficial fame, hypocrisy, and ultimate power, offering nothing but worldly promises in exchange for eternal imprisonment. Was this the end all be all to life? Was this the type of life I wanted for myself?

NO! No more! I refused to be a marionette puppet! No more trying to fit into what the

entertainment industry, or people, for that matter, wanted me to be! No more being teased by a dangling carrot! No more walking on eggshells to please others! No more tolerating the fake actor culture! NO MORE! My soul was not up for sale! For years, I pursued acting in the hopes of having my work exposed on a global scale, and for once in my life, I did not care! I didn't care about any of it!

I. WAS. DONE!

A gigantic iron hammer appeared and crushed the gilded cage—it instantly rotted away! Revved up from what had just happened, I turned my attention to the green pasture, stared at it with uncertainty, and yelled, "Fine! I'll take this one!" The image zipped right past my left shoulder and instantly disappeared!

Letting out a confession, I confided, "God, I don't care about fame, money, or status! My life feels small! I don't have a life! God, I want to live large! I want to live large with people!"

Just then ... everything in the apartment became ultra still, and almost instantly, I felt myself aligning with what seemed to be my soul's genuine desire. Something bigger was now calling me, and with that, I decided to ditch my life as "The Prince," and instead opted to be "The Pauper."

My horizons expanded exponentially while unconsciously seeking God through various Texas locals, both on and off the set—a domino effect: one minute, I'd be advised to read the Bible out loud to hear God speak to me, and the next, I'd find myself crying out snot after snot at a buddy's place, after being told to read from Psalms. These people seemed to know God; His majestic glow was written all over their faces, and I wanted what they had.

However, growing increasingly frustrated with hitting a dead end when it came to *experiencing* God ... left me yearning for more. Hanging out with believers was amazing, but

I was dying to know if someone had *met* Him. The only advice available was, "Read the Bible, and you'll know God through His word." But that wasn't good enough: my soul was parched, and my experience with God was not going to start and end with "Just read the Bible." Sorry ... no deal! A big part of my skeptical self still needed proof of His existence outside of scriptures, religious leaders, and pastors. Anyone could pick up a Bible and recite what's been written—that wasn't impressive to me. Although inspiring, scripture wasn't my endgame—where was God?

On one of my days off, I hopped off the transport van to watch a taping of *The Chosen,* when a familiar face caught my attention—Seth Trenda (he handed me the pink hard hat and vest on my previous visit to the site). And there it was again: that transparent light surrounding him and his men. It made no sense because these dudes looked like they could murder you in the middle of the night—*why did they seem "holy?"* It was such an odd contrast.

Filming was happening straight ahead, and the construction crew was off to my right. Where to go? Prompted toward the roughnecks, I ditched the set visit and boldly walked over to reintroduce myself to Seth. After giving him a handshake, we exchanged some quick words, and he returned to his office to finish up some work.

Moments later, the construction crew and I broke out into an impromptu (roundtable) discussion about *Experiences With God,* as more men left their workstations to join in. I shared with them my Lebanese origins and Grandpa Nickolas' spiritual influence on my life. They in turn shared their one-on-one experiences with God.

Seth eventually stepped out of his office with his brother-in-law Branden to find that his men were no longer working but, instead, had formed a semicircle around me, listening.

As I passionately talked about God saving my dad's life during his open-heart surgery, Seth and Branden were both struck with an idea! They quickly gave each other a look and turned back to face me. Seth offered, "Hey, our church is having a conference this weekend. You should come." The rest of the guys stared at me, curious as to what my response would be— can you say, *"awkward?"* Sensing a hesitation, Seth explained it was non-denominational, strictly focusing on God, Jesus, and the Holy Spirit.

Unsure about the invite and feeling like it may have been a plot to *kidnap* me (thanks, Aunt Sona), my wishy-washy response was an "Okay, I'll think about it." Seth and Branden darted looks at each other, turned their attention back to me, and in unison urged, *"We think you should come!"*

To ensure there would be no roadblocks to my showing up, Seth comped my ticket, and that was that—I was going!

It was the day of the church conference, but first, a much-needed pit stop would be made to join *The Chosen* crew for the lunch buffet.

On what was supposed to be a relaxing drive in the Midlothian hills, turned into an introspective, coming to terms with my misery and isolation. These truths were never allowed to surface consciously because they were too frightening to confront; years of pain had been left intact, and no true healing had taken place. It all lay dormant while pursuing an acting career: everything from my breakup to constant betrayals to disingenuous friendships and major let downs within the entertainment industry. It became tiring leading what felt like an empty life—on repeat! Twenty years of emotional beatdowns had left me joyless and broken.

At that moment, inspiration shed light on what I needed to admit to God. And as scary as it may have been, it was time to come to terms with this frightening truth.

While fearfully opening my mouth to speak out the confession, a bone-chilling *black hole* suddenly opened up right under my feet, and started swallowing me whole—something dark and external that wouldn't let go! It was DISGUSTINGLY DISTURBING! Attempting to shake it off was useless! This thing clung on tightly while *tornado-swirling* around my body, quickly moving its way up! (it was like Venom from *Spider-Man*).

My heart was racing! The dark being was super powerful—it had me in its clutches as it made its way to the top of my chest!

At that moment an innocent-sounding voice from inside me urgently warned, *"You have to tell God how you've been feeling right now. Admit it to Him. Tell Him quickly, or this is about to get bad."*

Just then, another dark being appeared externally in the passenger side seat and screeched in my ear, "Don't you DARE admit what you're about to admit!" I froze in complete shock—my body locked up! The innocent voice calmly chimed in again, *"Say it. Say it now."* The dark tornado-like being had reached the top of my chin and right when it was about to swallow me alive in this *all-hope-is-lost* moment, I cried out—"GOD! MY SOUL IS LOST!"

The dark being in the passenger side seat let out a bellowing scream as it instantly vanished along with the second dark being that had encapsulated my body!

Traumatized by the incident, the ugliest cry of my whole life was poured out! I was shattered, desperate to be saved by God! I didn't want to know Him by word of mouth, not even through scripture, or through being on a TV show! It was now or NEVER!

"GOD, I'VE HAD IT! I NEED WHAT YOU AND JESUS HAVE TO OFFER RIGHT NOW! PLEASE, GOD—I'M SCARED! I WANT A RELATIONSHIP WITH YOU DIRECTLY

AND I DON'T WANT ANYONE ELSE STANDING IN THE WAY! AND WHAT'S THE POINT OF THE HOLY SPIRIT!? WHAT IS IT SUPPOSED TO DO!? CAN YOU LET ME KNOW WHAT THE PURPOSE OF ALL OF THIS IS!!!?"

I was lost & desperately needed to be found. The only way to do that was for me to be a Middle Eastern "Karen" & ask to speak to the Manager of the entire universe directly!

I WAS READY TO MEET GOD!

Crowds of energized people rushed past me in excitement as they headed toward the Downtown Fort Worth Convention Center—*what was this, Disneyland?* Then there he was, standing in front of the building, Seth—in all his disarming, joyful glory. He outstretched his tatted arms and exclaimed, *"Heeey, man! I am glad you came! This is gonna be good!!!"* Unimpressed and completely disarmed from the madness that had just taken place moments ago, I hopelessly thought, *"If you say so."*

As we walked through the arena doors, the place looked more like Las Vegas than a church: front and center was a gigantic professionally lit stage with big screens on each side, accompanied by worship music. Thousands of people twirled around like ballerinas, and skipped about, while others took to their knees with arms outstretched above their heads. *What on earth*—growing up in the Greek Orthodox Church, we didn't exactly do backflips and twirls as part of our worship, so the whole thing caught me off guard. However, there was an overwhelming sense of absolute freedom and otherworldly love flowing everywhere, regardless of how odd the entire setup may have appeared to me.

Seth walked over to his brother-in-law Branden, who saved us seats with his family, as Branden's blonde-haired pageant-type wife rushed up to my face without warning and excitedly exclaimed, "Isn't He amazing!?" At first, I thought, *"Who are you talking about, lady?"* It took me a quick second to realize, *"Oh yeah, Jesus—good for you."* Her "over-the-top" enthusiasm went right over my head as Seth immediately remembered something—"Oh, you GOTTA meet Papa James!" He quickly darted off as I stood there wondering ... *"Who the heck is Papa James?"*

Not a moment later, Seth came marching back accompanied by an older, well-built gentleman named **James Orth** (a.k.a. "Papa James")—*His Superpower: intercessing.*

"Papa James" wore a short-sleeved button-down blue shirt, had white hair, and a thick white beard. In my mind, he looked like Papa Smurf from *The Smurfs*. James aggressively broke away from Seth, picked up his pace, and rushed at me before Seth could introduce us.

Then, as if being hit by some force field, James backed up a few steps after getting too close to me and was bewildered; he turned to Seth and revealed, "THIS is the guy you want me to meet!"

Turning his attention back to me, James commented, "Wow, you have a lot going on around you!" He blinked his eyes rapidly several times, leaned into my face, stared right into my soul, and exposed, "You are sick of where you've been living" (California had me feeling oppressed and isolated because of the lockdowns, and I was sick of living there). Utterly shocked, I turned to Seth, who put his hands up in defeat and confessed, "Hey man, I didn't tell him anything—he came to you before I could point you out."

James' anger built as he aggressively revealed, "All your life, your soul has been thirsty to go deep with people, and all you've been getting are little droplets of water where you live. But tonight, the floodgates are about to open, and you will go deeper with people than you've ever been. Tonight, you are going to MEET GOD."

"Papa Smurf" had completely disarmed and shocked me; how did he know all that? After he left to be with what I'm assuming were his other "Smurflings," the worship band took to the stage, and church ... was officially on!

While everyone around me was free-flowing to the live worship music like they were at Woodstock, my arms were crossed and my head was bowed. As I stood in isolation, completely lost, and desperate for a significant change in my life, the conference's atmosphere began to take me to a different place, and within minutes, an awareness of my entire family's burden came through. They were carrying something grey and heavy on their shoulders—a burden they had unknowingly transferred onto me: it encapsulated difficulties, fear, abandonment, anger, and a gut-wrenching immigration process that I bore witness to as a child.

From within myself, I wholeheartedly begged ... "God, please lift this heaviness that's been on me and my family. I don't want it anymore." About ten minutes later, there was a jarring tap on my shoulder—it was Seth's son; he leaned in and said, "I was praying for you from back there (a good distance away), and God told me to tell you that by showing up tonight, you've broken your family's generational curse." Shocked and overtaken with grief, I broke down and felt the burden lift right off as we embraced; it was unbelievable!

SERMON TIME!

Up popped on stage a blond, boisterous pastor who could arguably win the award for "The Most Emotionally Passionate Person on Planet Earth!" Every word she spoke had intensity and conviction as she screamed-talked her sermons relentlessly! Leaning over to Seth I commented, "Dude, she's the female version of Steven Tyler from *Aerosmith.*" Seth stared at me with the look of *crazy* etched all over his face and let a short-lived chuckle escape him, as I officially dubbed her, "Pastor Steven Tyler."

During the sermon, the pastor stunned me with a proclamation that hit too close to home. Seemingly out of the blue, she manically screamed to the entire arena, "Tonight ... YOU, are going to be a TRANSFORMER WARRIOR! Tonight, you will TRANSFORM! YOU ... are a **TRANSFORMER!!!**"

"WHAT...? TRANSFORMER!?—was anyone else hearing this!?"

"Pastor Steven Tyler" then introduced a concept I had never heard of: *burying your idols.* We were to get on our knees and give to God everything we had put above Him.

Hoards of people took to the floor and bowed their heads as my smugness claimed, *"I don't have any idols."* Not a second later, that familiar Fatherly voice came through to challenge, "Yeah, you do. Your mom, your dad, your sisters, your acting gigs, your voice-overs, your brother-in-law, your other sister's fiancé, your Jeep, and your bank accounts—you've put all these things before Me."

Realizing that God was last in my life instantly pierced my heart; pride had to go; in fact, it needed to be buried. Humbly getting down on one knee, I gently placed a hand on the floor and in defeat, bowed my head apologetically; there was a coming to terms with God, that needed to happen—a reconciliation of my being so distant from Him, and for not allowing Him into my life altogether—for putting Him *last*.

The weight of this world had crushed me, and I no longer wanted any part of it; it was the end of the line—as if being backed into a dark alley with nowhere left to turn.

My sisters had moved on with their lives, my parents were retired, and the constant theme of being left out in the cold by disingenuous, backstabbing people had done me in—where was **my** place in this world? Where did I belong? The answer seemed to be ... *nowhere.* The world, with all its false promises, had nothing left that it could offer me, so ... I buried all my idols to God. As long as I could be with Him, giving it all up would be worth it, even if it meant never seeing my own family again.

My eyes opened and the conference was over; *how long was I "out?"* While feeling loopy yet uplifted, I thanked Seth and Branden for having invited me as thousands of people shuffled out of the convention center.

Then, a familiar face rounded the corner from a distance—James *("Papa Smurf")* hectically weaved through the crowd, making his way over. He took out a vial of anointing oil and confirmed, "Ah, good, you're still here. God told me you'd still be here—*now, hold out your hands!"*

Having nothing left to lose, I followed suit as James drew crosses on my palms and right in the middle of my forehead using the anointing oil (Grandpa used to do this after baptizing babies, so it wasn't a completely foreign concept).

James placed his palms over mine and spoke in what sounded like an indistinguishable language: they called it, *"Speaking In Tongues."* Seth, Branden, and their families crept in without warning, gently placing their hands all over me as they began speaking in their version of "tongues" when...

SPARKS!

Electricity and radiation ignited and pulsated throughout my entire body!

PRESENCE!

It was a physiological reaction to a stimulus outside myself—I could sense every one of my cells vibrating at warp speed as an overflow of otherworldly LOVE took complete control of my body! I was in shock and tried to escape but my feet were stuck to the floor—I couldn't move my body! Then ...

GOD

He rose, expanding outward in front of my very eyes like a transparent forcefield and enveloped the ENTIRE convention center, towering above it—revealing Himself as a truly larger-than-life being! Talk about an entrance!

I. COULD. NOT. BELIEVE. IT!!!

He was right there in front of me! God! My Lord! My Savior! My EVERYTHING! And man, He was NOT what I thought He would be! There was no putting into words what God / Jesus Christ / Holy Spirit looked like; He was transparent, yet visible, formless, but with a strong Fatherly presence! He radiated His unlimited power EVERYWHERE!

IT WAS HIM!

All-encompassing, all-knowing, all ruling, all EVERYTHING! And I mean ... **EVERYTHING!!!** The experience was frightening—meeting God was nothing like meeting a human—not even close! My entire body couldn't help but react on a molecular level to being in the presence of its Creator! I could not believe what was happening!

"RADIOACTIVE LOVEFIRE"

That's the only way I can describe His love! It penetrated my body and almost made me lose my mind—it felt AMAZING!!!!!!! He was wondrous, spectacular, shocking, and I can't say this enough—**EVERYTHING!!!!!!** His presence overwhelmed me to the point of almost losing consciousness—my body couldn't handle being in the presence of such majestic perfection!

Right as I was about to pass out from an overwhelming sense of unworthiness, He shot a piece of Himself into me, and this time, His RADIOACTIVE LOVEFIRE set ablaze my entire body, starting at the bottom of my feet, all the way up to my chin! By the time that RADIOACTIVE LOVEFIRE surpassed the top of my head, I experienced the frightening sensation of passing away for a brief moment! Then after a split second, I was brought back to life, in a state of "undead" (or *"Zombie Nick,"* as I call it).

While drowning in awe, the sensation of being submerged in water engulfed me, causing a floating sensation as the prayers continued. Then, without warning, the protective oceanic liquid bubble encapsulating me erupted!

Instantaneously, James' eyes flung open! He immediately took his hand off my chest— everyone else followed suit.

Pulsating with ultimate power, I stood there blessed, grounded, and filled with supernatural love and an unshakable certainty! James looked deep into my eyes, squinted, and said, "You've received the Holy Spirit—He's in you now." Explaining to him that it already happened when Grandpa baptized me, prompted James to respond, "Sure. The Spirit may have been resting on you. But now He's resting IN you." "Papa Smurf" wasn't lying; I could sense the presence of what Jesus called, *The Holy Spirit.*" He gripped me through the center of my abdomen as He simultaneously surrounded me from all corners and radiated a flow of love through me! Holy Spirit was just as real as anyone in that convention center; I couldn't believe what had happened!

I. MET. GOD!

Now that the Holy Spirit was in me, James put me on the spot, claiming I could *speak in tongues.* He aggressively challenged me to do so but I didn't even want to go there. Taking on a more intimidating stance, James encouraged,

"COME ON! It's the spiritual language you use to communicate with the Lord!"

After watching him speak in his *tongues* for a brief moment, my tongue erupted outside my control the second my mouth was opened, and the next thing I knew, my body experienced the sensation of being caught on fire as I began speaking in new ways! The Holy Spirit took over, and it was *dizzying*—as if a radioactive power plant was shoved into the pit of my stomach, dispersing unlimited energy to all corners of my body, inflating me to the point of an epic explosion! After the infusion of power had reached its climax, everything came to a sudden halt!

James stared into my eyes and proclaimed, "Your voice is no longer yours; it belongs to Him. From now on, He will speak through you." James then pointed at my chest and claimed, "... and because you have the same heart that Jesus did, you will touch people, and they will heal; you will cast out demons in His name, and you will have all the same spiritual giftings that Jesus did."

I stood there, not wanting to move an inch. The Holy Spirit's presence was intense yet gentle—I basked in it. Seth stood at a distance, staring on ecstatically. He then commented, "Dude, you look so different! Your family is going to freak out when you go back to California... They aren't going to recognize you."

EIGHTEEN

HUNGRY

I was reeling all weekend from what had happened at the church conference on Friday; pain, anger, and doubt had been removed from my body, and it was odd to be in such a state of well-being. Never in a million years would I have believed that years of accumulated trauma and burdens could have been wiped away within seconds—SECONDS!

Word spread about my encounter among the construction crew on set, and they, along with their friends, threw a surprise homemade pizza get-together in honor of my having received the Holy Spirit. You gotta love Texans and their generosity of spirit! It was good pizza, too—three different kinds, to be exact!

As William (one of the construction guys) opened the door to his duplex condo unit, a group of people roared and cheered loudly from the dinner table as I pushed back, "Okay, guys, enough. Now you're making me feel like I joined a cult"—to which they burst into cultish-like laughter.

Breaking bread with these complete "strangers" was surreal because they felt familiar—like I had already known them. The radiance they emanated was so intense—that "highlighter" effect.

Jeremiah (another construction guy) sat across the table from me, revealing a very unexpected backstory to my encounter. He inquired, "Do you know where my workstation was based?" Jeremiah teared up as he revealed, "In YOUR house, Zebedee's house." He was the one who started writing scripture on the walls of the set, after having heard from God to do so.

Jeremiah explained, "It all started in Zebedee's house, and that's what inspired the other workers to write scripture on the walls of the homes they'd been working on. This all started with you! I don't think it's an accident that you're sitting across the table from me today so that I could tell you this."

My chest welled up—it was too much to take in. The original trek to Texas involved my begrudgingly booking *The Chosen* ... and now God was pinpointing Zebedee's house, signaling the encounter that the actor would have with Him!?

Time flew by—a good night's rest was needed before filming my final scene the next day (Zebedee buying the olive grove). As I stood up ready to leave, Jeremiah hopped right out of his chair, walked over, and embraced me like a kid hugging Santa Claus. He then asked if he could pray for me, to which I pointed out, "Sure, go for it ... that seems to be an ongoing theme with you Texans." Everyone laughed as

Jeremiah placed both hands on my shoulders, put his head down, and said a beautiful prayer that ended with "... and Lord, may Nick come to know you more through fasting."

A visceral laughter erupted from me, which confused the group, including Jeremiah. I clarified, "Really, thank you bro, but you picked the wrong guy for that fasting prayer. I'm the guy who shows up to set on my days off for the lunch buffet."

MY TRAP WOULDN'T STAY SHUT!

Getting into everyone's faces, screaming about God, Jesus, and the Holy Spirit must have made me look like a lunatic, but who cared!? The cast and crew's reactions—confusion, shock, disbelief, fear, and intrigue all wrapped up into one, as they all heard one name being screamed repeatedly; "JESUS! JESUS! JESUS!" Keeping quiet was not an option! "Everything He talked about is TRUE! HE'S REAL!!!!! The HOLY SPIRIT ... WOW! That FIRE! Oh, MAN, that

FIRE!!!!! It was INSANE! Oh! Then ... I DIED ... but I came back to LIFE! *Crazy weekend, huh!?"* The cast and crew were dumbfounded!

After a few hours of shooting, it was time for lunch, and my to-go box was loaded with a heaping pile of food, even on the lid side. Jalein and Chris (our behind-the-scenes hosts) sat across from me at the cafeteria table and were shocked to hear more than an earful about my encounter with God.

What was more shocking by the end of lunch was the state of the to-go box; the food on one side was halfway eaten while the lid portion remained untouched. Lunch was over, and as everyone headed back to set, I sat there, staring at all the remaining food—*weird*. After returning to my apartment that evening, the to-go box was tossed into the fridge.

I had two days off before my flight back to California, so the plan was to crash lunch for those remaining days. But this time, only one side of the to-go container would be filled since my appetite seemed to have shrunk. While sitting back in the chair, confusion set in—I could barely finish half of what was loaded onto the container.

Sitting across from me, Chris even noticed and asked, "Aren't you going to at least get dessert?" I sat back, thinking it may have been the flu.

Returning to the apartment that evening, I opened the fridge to store the leftovers and spotted the to-go container from the previous day ... it remained untouched. After staring at it momentarily, I placed the second container beside it and shut the fridge door.

It was the final day of shooting; Chris and Jalein sat across from me in the cafeteria as I opted to eat off of a paper plate instead of a sizeable to-go container—my appetite was virtually nonexistent. Chris asked, "Is that all you're having?"—a tiny serving of chicken, salad, and a baby-sized portion of rice. I admitted,

"Yeah, I haven't been feeling hungry lately for some reason." THEN—a realization: *"Jeremiah's fasting prayer!? NO! There was no way! The Holy Spirit Diet!?"* I couldn't believe what had happened; the sensation of needing physical nourishment was eradicated from my body! Hunger and thirst were gone!

NINETEEN

REVELATIONS

As I hung out near the set, a white pickup truck pulled up alongside the dirt road and came to a sudden stop. Inside was who I call "Mr. Grins A-Lot." Throughout my time on location, this dude would be seated on top of his UTV in the middle of a grass field, smiling and waving at me. *"What's that guy's deal?"* I'd always think.

"Mr. Grins A-Lot" immediately exited his truck, grabbed something from a nearby workstation, and as he got back into his vehicle to pull out, my hand darted right up, pointed at him, and I barked, "Hey, you!" He lowered his passenger side window, tilted his head down, and there it was again ... that friendly smile.

He asked, "Hey man, were you at the (church) conference this weekend?" I curiously answered, "Yeah, I was ... were you?" "Mr. Grins A-Lot" nodded, smiled again, and admitted, "Yuuup!"

He placed his truck into park, immediately jumped out, and ran toward the front of the hood, where we collided in an explosive hug! "Dude, what's your name?" I awkwardly asked. He laughed and said, "Oh, I'm Michael," then we both laughed. **Michael Singh**—*His Superpower: making anyone love him.*

Michael was over the moon for my newly found relationship with God as he had had revelations with the Holy Spirit. "You know what's interesting?" I asked. "A cousin of mine said that my guardian angel is Michael, and whenever the colors purple and gold are prominent, he's around." Signaling Michael's sunglass visor, I pointed out its purple and gold tint. He smiled and revealed, "I *do* know jujitsu."

After chatting briefly, we exchanged numbers and gave each other a *see ya later.*

Shortly after he took off, Michael texted asking if I'd join him and his friend/co-worker John for dinner at Prime 115 Steakhouse that evening to discuss some things. The restaurant's name resonated with me for obvious reasons, so I accepted!

Prime 115 looked like a mafia hangout. Michael was sitting at a table, still in his construction attire, and to his left was his buddy and co-worker, **John Hart**. John was big and burly, a no-nonsense kind of guy. He sported a dirty baseball hat, and dirt-ridden construction attire to match—*His Superpower: unapologetically loving & honest.*

After joining them at the table, it was apparent how much John loved and knew God; he shared his Holy Spirit experience, and we instantly bonded.

As steaks were served with stir-fried shiitake Brussels sprouts and gourmet mashed potatoes, John asked, "Have you seen the video about how we wrote scripture on the walls of the set of *The Chosen?*" I answered, "Yeah, Jeremiah told me about how he heard from God to start doing that in Zebedee's house."

That was that, there was nothing else John could have added to surprise me; at least, that's what I thought anyway. His voice shifted and became slightly shakier as tears flooded his eyes. After collecting himself, John revealed, "I don't know if you knew this, but before we broke ground, we got together as a crew and prayed for one of the actors to receive the Holy Spirit ... and that this actor would be the seed who would spread the gospel all over..."

I stopped eating ... and looked at John— he locked eyes with me. I couldn't say a single word. Our silent stare at one another communicated everything that needed to be said; things were getting stranger by the second.

As I slowly turned my attention to Michael in paranoia, he was grinning from ear to ear, nodding and saying his loveably agreeable catchphrase, "Yuup ... Yuuup!"

This was all too much: Antonia Reed ("The Oracle"), Seth Trenda's conference invite, James Orth ("Papa Smurf"), Jeremiah ("Fasting Prayer Bro") ... and now THIS!?

Turning back to John, I leaned across the table, and argued, "Okay, this was all very interesting, but you got the wrong guy—I'm not some preacher, and I'm not spreading any gospel. Also as a side note, this isn't *The Matrix*—I am not your 'Neo,' and you are not my 'Morpheus,' okay!? I'm not doing it!"

Honestly, I didn't feel *good enough* to carry everything being thrown at me—who was I to have received so much, anyway? My life experience for the past 20 years consisted of being belittled and tossed aside by people around the clock. And now what ...? All of a sudden I was being brought front and center while being showered with love, kindness, and respect!? IT MADE ZERO SENSE!

John honestly didn't care what I thought—he nodded with unshakable certainty and affirmed, "Yes, you are," to my, "No I'm not."

Meanwhile, Michael could not keep his darn trap shut with that ear-to-ear grin! He chimed in once again, "Yuup ... Yuuup!" These were good dudes—I liked them, but they were freaking me out!

Like ... *why ME?*

While leaning back in my chair, that familiar Fatherly voice reaffirmed, "I want you to Spiritually Battle." The directive sank into my being, and immediately, there was a sense to oblige.

Bringing my attention back to John, I repeated, "I heard God say He wants me to *'Spiritually Battle.'*" Without hesitation, John confidently removed his black silicone bracelet inscribed with The Full Armor of God scripture and handed it to me. He said, "Here, this is for your battle."

The directive was loud and clear: God wanted me to start helping people...

We ended the night with big goodbye hugs outside Prime 115. What a crazy adventure Texas had been; there was still so much to talk about and much more to understand—saying goodbye felt so premature.

In less than 24 hours, I'd be on a flight back to California, where all the people I knew and loved, would find it hard to recognize who they once knew ... as *"Nick."*

TWENTY

SPIRITUAL BACKLASH

My entire family lost it! They were worried about me and could sense an undeniable change had occurred. All I could do was talk about my encounter with God and the Holy Spirit; I could not shut up, and no one could shut me up. It was Jesus this and Jesus that and JESUS JESUS JESUS! Wait, let me write that one more time ... JESUS! Gosh, I love saying His name!

Mom took it the hardest—after all, I *was* her baby, and she could barely recognize me. I'd unabashedly say, "He's in me and all around me! I can sense Him! I can sense Him! He's here right now!" Mom almost had a full-on panic attack, wondering what happened to the moody son she once knew.

On one of my tirades, Mom cut me off mid-sentence and yelled, "Enough already! Stop talking about Jesus! SEE what you're doing? You're making me blaspheme!" Dad, on the other hand, was semi-cool—brushing it off as a blessing—he didn't seem too worried. Meanwhile, Mom seriously thought I had joined a cult. Who could blame her? She kept having to hear, "I encountered God! It was at this church conference where people prayed over me in tongues! You know ... *tongues!?*" (as if the poor woman did). Mom looked at me like I was an idiot and claimed, "They brainwashed you." Eventually, she would come around ... *kinda*.

Honestly, the brakes needed to be pumped on my intensity, but I couldn't help it! How could I have possibly stayed quiet after experiencing God and having been saved from years of darkness!?

The Holy Spirit's love flowed intensely through me and all around me 24/7, and most people didn't seem to get it.

It wasn't only what was being said that received side-eyed looks from family; my entire demeanor had changed: while hanging out with my cousin Lara, she remarked, "Your face looks different." To which I revealed, "It's the Holy Spirit!" Lara analytically squinted her eyes and in slight paranoia responded, "That's weird..."

My unrelenting desire to continuously talk about God, Jesus, and the Holy Spirit simultaneously caused a lot of friction and upheaval everywhere I went, including a religious leader aggressively accusing me of being possessed by a demon, claiming that the Holy Spirit encounter and spiritual giftings started and ended with Jesus' disciples. My smart-aleck response was, "Well if this is a demon, then he's got an identity crisis going on because all I've been doing is talking about Jesus."

The backlash wouldn't stop, and sometimes it came in unexpected ways: an acquaintance whose life turned around in miraculous ways after my having performed a proclamation over his head, verbally attacked me just weeks later with claims of egotistical motives behind what I was doing—he didn't get it. Upon hearing this, I sat there in disbelief.

Nevertheless, it was time to move on and keep going! Everyone had to know about Him! Why? No man, guru, philosophy, or self-help book could have brought me out of darkness the way God, Jesus Christ, and the Holy Spirit did. NO ONE—BUT HIM! God, Jesus Christ, and the Holy Spirit! And, of course ... Grandpa. There's no doubt that he was also instrumental in all of this!

MORE PEOPLE MUST KNOW!

An impromptu road trip was taken to Los Angeles, and I was most excited about visiting with cousin Seta at her alteration shop; she was the one who would rave about Jesus to all her customers. The story of my encounter could have gone either way with Seta, so I braced myself for the worst.

After scarfing down my last slice of pizza in her alteration shop, I told Seta everything. She remained utterly silent while critically examining me from head to toe with only her eyes and with arms crossed militantly.

Seta then bluntly admitted—*"Same thing happened to me."*

My eyes bugged out—I jumped forward, yelling, "REALLY?! NO!!!" Seta jumped right back, screaming, "Of course!!! A pastor prayed over me in a language I didn't understand— the fire covered my entire body, and I fell to my knees, begging him to call 911—I felt like I was dying!"

FINALLY!

Someone in the family who knew EXACTLY what I was talking about! Then ... a major realization—"Wait! Is that why you're so fearless about Jesus with your customers!? Oh! Was THAT why I was so drawn to your shop back in the day!? It was because of Him!?" Seta antagonistically leaned forward, got in my face, and passionately lectured, "Of course it was Him! Who am I for it to be me!? ARE YOU KIDDING ME!? Who am I??? Who are you??? Pff! OF COURSE IT'S JESUS, COME ON! ARE, YOU, KIDDING, ME!!??"

Seta knew Him! And now that I was in the presence of someone who did ... a no-holds-barred conversation would commence while chatting up a storm about the All Almighty. However, little did I know ... that my initial encounter with God / Jesus Christ / Holy Spirit ... would be the first of many.

TWENTY ONE

AMAZING ACTS UNBELIEVABLE ENCOUNTERS

*This chapter is dedicated to you,
God, Jesus Christ, & the Holy Spirit.
And to my Grandfather Nickolas for leaving
behind your spiritual footprints that lead
me to our Creator.*

If you had told me that one day I'd be writing an autobiography that led to a God encounter, I'd probably get a real kick out of it & bust out laughing. After all, I was the one who poked fun at all the "Jesus-type" folk and their "over-the-top" passion for Him.

Upon my return to film Season 4 of The Chosen, a swag box was left on the kitchen counter of the apartment as a welcome gift. Inside was everything from a hat to a mug to a shirt, showcasing some form of The Chosen emblem.

One particular item caught my attention—a simple black notebook with the fish logo etched onto it. As it was held in my hand, that resounding Fatherly voice ordered, "You will write down everything that happens to you, here."

The following is a replica of journal entries after each encounter & act.
More information has been added for clarification & elaboration purposes.

TEXAS, JOHN'S HOUSE:
THURSDAY, APRIL 6, 2023

My buddy John ("Morpheus") and I spent a lot of time catching up and chatting about God on his living room couch. He let me know there was scripture written all over the dry walls of his home. An urge came to me that I had to give something to this house in the name of the Lord. In Arabic, I prayed the Our Father prayer for his family and the house. The words flew out of my mouth; they continuously changed color from golden orange to neon red, then reunited, merging with the English scriptures written on the walls. After finishing, I looked up and told John I could see my words soaking into the English scriptures, activating them. John did not seem surprised, he agreed. Before I could finish my thought, he interjected, "...and it glowed an orange color as it got activated?" I said, "Yeah! I was just about to say that! A neon orangish-red." John said he saw the same thing happen. We both paused and laughed.

TEXAS, FREEWAY:
FRIDAY, APRIL 7, 2023

On Good Friday, I was invited to a Seder dinner. While driving on the freeway, the presence of the Holy Spirit suddenly fogged up my entire car with blinding light and overwhelmed me with His ever-present illumination and warmth. I could sense Him resting intensely on the outside of my chest and all around me; it felt like a grandeur embrace, an expression of His unconditionally ardent love that was unbearably good. It was indescribable, this sincere love that was beyond amazing, causing my chest to feel like it was about to cave in. I started giggling uncontrollably and screamed out, "What you gave me last time wasn't enough, God! I want more of Jesus and the Holy Spirit! Give me more than I can stand!" The brightness intensified, and the entire freeway glowed with golden white light!

TEXAS, CHURCH: RESURRECTION DAY
SUNDAY, APRIL 9, 2023

I met up at church with Seth and Branden's families and experienced such a profound full-circle moment while standing there with my head bowed. Even though the place was vast and full of attendees, I only sensed an intense oneness with God; it was just us: this sense of inundating unity made me cry. As my eyes were closed, images of my relatives started swirling around in space. Light shot from one to the next, healing each of them.

My attention was brought back to church after a gentleman from earlier, who recognized me from The Chosen, came up from behind, wrapping his arm around my shoulder, letting me know he was praying for me. He wanted to relay a message from God. He said, "God wants you to know that when you cried out to tell Him what He gave you wasn't enough ... He heard you. He heard you when you said you wanted more of the Holy Spirit and Jesus ... and wants you to know that He's going to give you more than you can handle very soon."

TEXAS, APARTMENT:
THURSDAY, APRIL 13, 2023

While on a WhatsApp video call with my cousin Caroline in Greece, she opened up to me about a relative who had placed a curse on her mom a long time ago while she was pregnant with her. Because of this curse, my cousin had always experienced a dark, challenging life, just like her mom. After transitioning over to the subject of her son's recent trip to the barber, a Holy Being's presence came raining down through the top of my head. It flooded the center of my chest with an overwhelming amount of golden fire as it profusely overflowed inside me, filled the center of my chest, and spilled out of my eyes. As I stared at Caroline on my phone, I could see shimmering golden curtains appear around her. Stopping her abruptly in the middle of her story,

I sensed the urgency to return to the subject of her family curse and offered immediately to break it.

While still on camera, Caroline immediately took to the floor on her knees, bowed her head in desperation, and closed her eyes. I waited to see what the Holy Figure would compel me to do. I could almost see how dark, moldy, and devastating the curse was. It was heinously thick and evil. And the fact that this malicious curse thought it could overpower Jesus Christ got me worked up and ready to fire away! I found myself intensely screaming out a proclamation while flailing my arm like a madman, with my eyes closed and head bobbing rapidly left and right. My screaming ended abruptly with an "In the name of Jesus Christ, Amen!" I opened my eyes and looked at Caroline, who slowly lifted her head and sobbed a desperate "Thank you." I told her I could see the image of cracks forming on her face and explained that the curse had received a significant punch. It wasn't broken yet, but something would break very soon.

Caroline thanked me and said that her apartment suddenly felt different. She eventually got back to finishing her son's barber visit story and how she generously tipped the barber an amount equivalent to a haircut when ... I heard a "Thank you for doing that" come through from above me. Without hesitation, I cut Caroline off by repeating what I had just heard—"Thank you for doing that." Caroline paused and was stunned. She asked, "How did you know I was about to say that?" She went on to explain the ending to her story ... her son's barber telling her, "Thank you for that" (a reaction to her generous tip). I was now the one who was stunned and told her it was what I heard a Fatherly voice say right after the proclamation was completed.

The rays of light still showering through my head suddenly morphed into a tangible human form that was now warmly hugging me from behind, with comforting radiant arms wrapped around my chest. I said, "Oh my gosh, he's right behind me! IIe's hugging me from behind, and his head is resting on mine!" Caroline replied, stunned, "WOW." As the hug got tighter, the apartment kitchen got brighter and brighter. My eyes couldn't take that level of perfection being emitted. I began to be filled with a new level of love much more potent than the initial encounter at the church conference months prior. "I have to go; this is getting too intense!" I begged Caroline. She said, "Okay, call me later. I want to make sure everything is okay."

The second I hung up, the Holy Being's fingertips dipped right into the center of my chest and flooded my entire body with golden beams of fire and light. Fireworks burst right through my eyes, like Cyclops from X-Men. It felt like my pupils were about to be burned off! I was going blind and had lost complete control of my entire body. The whole apartment started to vibrate at an intensely uncontrollable frequency! Everything sparkled, blurred, and had life in it—the apartment, the kitchen, the furniture—

everything! The high-frequency vibration was so intense that the physical world around me began to fade away in the presence of this otherworldly figure. The hands pressed deeper into my chest, and at that moment, I could have just died. I kept eyeing my phone, sensing that 911 may need to be dialed at any second.

The sensation was like being on a nonstop roller coaster drop while not wearing a seat belt. I screamed out, begging, "No, no, God, please, no! That's enough! PLEASE STOP!!! I can't take it anymore!" I could feel every atom and molecule in my body vibrating at a rapidly unstable rate because of the external stimulus of His presence. It felt like I was about to be torn apart in the most loving way. I pushed the bar stool aside and found myself being forced down onto my knees by rays of golden radioactive light that rained down all over my head and back. Being gravitated to the floor, I cried out in sheer joy, ecstasy, and wonder. I couldn't remain standing due to the majestic presence of His supernatural royalty—His Highness. It was FRIGHTENING! The physical world around me became unstable in this Holy Being's presence. The earthly "reality" paled compared to what this heavenly reality was ushering in. The apartment and everything in it wasn't as "real" as I thought it might have been because I was in an extramundane realm of existence in His divine presence. Everything looked like it was about to evaporate before my eyes, including myself.

While crouched down on my knees, I placed my forehead down on the kitchen floor and desperately cried for it all to stop. In a last-ditch effort, I begged, PLEASE GOD! PLEASE STOP! THIS IS TOO MUCH. I CAN'T TAKE IT ANYMORE! IT'S TOO MUCH LOVE. I LOVE YOU, I LOVE YOU, I LOVE YOU!" I burst into more tears. I could sense myself being wiped out of existence as I began to blend in with the atmosphere around me. The more Radioactive Lovefire He poured into and over me, the more it seemed like I was about to be erased.

The apartment stabilized and pulsated with robust vibrancy as I reached my breaking point. Then, a hand was placed on top of my head, which froze me in shock, and it remained there for what felt like forever. I was too afraid to look up, so I kept my eyes on the floor, where I saw two feet wearing sandals and draped in a robe. The figure was a monochromatic pearl with reflections of pink and yellowish-blue tints. Suddenly, the hand was gone, and so was the figure. He reappeared behind me as I nervously waited for what would happen next. I felt Him gently grab my right arm and slowly lift me from the ground. Then, the most comforting cloth I'd ever felt was gently draped over my head and shoulders, reaching way down to the middle of my back. It was as real and tangible as any article of clothing I'd ever worn and felt heavenly, soft, comforting, loving, and light. The figure vanished, leaving behind tingles of where the cloth was draped, as this celestial sensation lingered for the rest of the day. No matter where I looked, it was beautifully vivid, vibrant, and pulsating with what can only be described as "High-Frequency-Life."

TEXAS, APARTMENT BEDROOM: SATURDAY, APRIL 15, 2023

In the middle of the night, a WhatsApp text came from my cousin Caroline in Greece. She sent me a picture of her sturdy wooden chandelier that had crashed onto her dining room table early in the morning. Out of seven mason jars that were attached to it, one had shattered into pieces. She said that the sound of the blast was apocalyptically explosive, as she woke up startled. This happened just hours after our video call. In the text, she asked, "Is this what you meant by something breaking soon?"—referring to the proclamation I made just a few hours prior, for her family curse. My eyes widened as Caroline said she felt something leave her apartment that evening, causing the atmosphere to feel lighter. She sensed that the curse had finally broken.

Caroline curiously asked what I was doing while this incident occurred simultaneously in her apartment. I responded, "I went to an ice cream shop that advertised serving their sundaes in glass mason jars."

TEXAS, APARTMENT BEDROOM:
THURSDAY, APRIL 27, 2023

I woke up in bed and could tangibly feel a protective shield around my chest and a heavy-duty helmet on my head. They radiated love and lightness and were impenetrable. Their appearance was slightly transparent, with a diamond-like quality that shimmered with circular blue orbs.

TEXAS, APARTMENT BEDROOM:
FRIDAY, APRIL 28, 2023

While taking a small nap before visiting the set, I sensed very comforting boots appear on my bare feet. They were warm and padded with blue bubble insoles that gave them a bounce.

TEXAS, APARTMENT KITCHEN:
MONDAY, MAY 1, 2023

While sharing my intense encounters over the phone with my cousin Zepure, who lived in LA, she opened up to me about a curse that had been taking the lives of young men in her family when they reached their 20s. As my cousin told me about a burning coal curse that her grandfather's former lover used to curse his male lineage, my entire apartment brightened up with that blinding light. As I looked around, the walls were dripping with molten gold. I sensed a directive to break the curse. I quickly cut my cousin off to let her know what was happening and what I was about to do. She remained quiet on the other end of the line while I waited on God. With a sudden rush of musical energy, I found myself belting out a ballad in the name of Jesus Christ. The melody *was one that I had never heard before. The ballad flowed effortlessly like it was putting to bed and softly bunting the curse out of my cousin's life.*

The song ended, and my cousin remained silent. Then, she sobbed and thanked me with a tone of relief. I reflected for a moment and relayed to her that it was over. The multi-generational curse had been broken. I really could sense it. She said, "You know how I know what you did is confirmation from God? Only my immediate family knows this ... I have a saying ... Music Is Life." She asked, "Have you ever sung for anyone else as a prayer?" I responded with, "Uh—NO." I realized then that my "prayers" for people would be in the form of God lead proclamations.

TEXAS, APARTMENT:
FRIDAY, MAY 5, 2023

That deep, comforting, Fatherly voice came through to tell me: "All people have to do is stop not believing." Because all things were created through Jesus, including people, He is already a part of us. He is in our DNA. By denying Him, we are denying a part of who we are.

TEXAS, APARTMENT:
FRIDAY, MAY 5, 2023

I asked God to fill me with more of the Holy Spirit—to remove more of me and add more of Him. About an hour later, the entire apartment was filled with light, and I felt God filling me with that Radioactive Lovefire again. When I went to set, I waited for our makeup artist, who walked in late after getting a cortisone shot in her toe. While whitening my beard, she struggled with the throbbing pain. God's directive caught me off guard and infused me with an order to touch her toe, count down from 10 to 1, and do it in the name of Jesus Christ. It sounded like such a bizarre directive, but I followed through.

I told the makeup artist to stop whitening my beard and, with urgency, asked if I could touch her toe. She let me, so I bent down while still in the makeup chair, placed my fingers gently over the toe area of her shoe, and softly counted down: 10, 9, 8, 7, 6, 5, 4, 3, 2, 1, and proclaimed it in the name of Jesus Christ. Instantly stunned, she looked at the other makeup artist with tears and announced, "... it worked!" I was floored and asked her if she was messing with me. She responded excitedly and tearfully, "I'm not kidding, Nick, it worked! I mean ... the throbbing is still there, but the pain is gone! I was about to let out a scream a split second before you touched it!"

TEXAS, APARTMENT BEDROOM:
TUESDAY, MAY 23, 2023

I was jolted with a burst of playful energy in the center of my chest! It was in the middle of the night, and an excitable childlike force woke me from a deep sleep. I opened my eyes to find a swarm of what appeared to be Angelic beings flying elegantly around the ceiling in one gigantic circular motion. There must have been at least 50 of them, layered one on top of the other, making it hard to pinpoint the exact number of them present. Visually, they were completely transparent, slender, and elongated in shape. I couldn't see their faces. They were wondrous and shocking ... playful and childlike but with the swiftness of a world-class ballerina and the strength of a warrior who could effortlessly slice you in half!

Some flew down, surrounding me, and I quickly sat up. Then they tugged at me playfully, urging me to go with them as I sat there in awe, not believing what was happening. I thought, "Okay, okay, I'm coming, I'm coming." I didn't want to risk making these Angelic beings angry, so I jumped out of bed and walked around the apartment in absolute amazement, as they flew past me in droves, circled, and swirled right back while performing inversions.

I could feel their perfect breeze as they flew by and soared over my head. The time on the stovetop was 3:20 am. These Angelic beings formed a *circular tunnel right in front of me. I was hesitant, but they didn't seem to pose any threat, so I began walking through the tunnel they created. The more I walked through the tunnel, the more I could sense my feet almost being lifted off the ground. It was like a celebration. Realizing how crazy and intense this was and questioning why I was entertaining it, I excused myself and went straight to bed. They wouldn't leave me alone. The Angelic beings continued hovering around the ceiling in excited anticipation of fun and play. It took what seemed like almost an hour for me to fall back to sleep as they all continually hovered above my bed while infusing the center of my chest with fire and excitement.*

Many encounters & acts took place
beyond what is written here: everything from
Jesus sitting across from me on my bed, while
circulating glowing, blue orbs on my palms,
to countless encounters with God, & the
Holy Spirit. If I had to list everything,
it would make for one long book.

It was a blessing to have experienced
God's heavenly realm;
I had finally come to know Him.

Yet ... one issue remained: I still didn't know me.
However, God, being all-knowing,
all-powerful, & all-loving, wouldn't allow
my life's story to go down like that;
He was about to hand me back something
I had lost a long time ago...

TWENTY TWO

THE ANOINTED TOW TRUCK LADY

Upon my return to California, much time was spent reflecting on everything that had transpired throughout my life leading up to the encounter. After spending nearly two years with God, there were many wonders He performed that I bore witness to; it turned out that His acts weren't limited to just the Bible as some had claimed.

I'd mention an experience to a believer and would be met with, "Be careful, man ... make sure it lines up with scripture."

Being told to disregard God's work in our present time if *scripture* didn't mention it didn't exactly gel with me. Although well-intentioned, some were attempting to place me in a new kind of cage, a cage of their ironclad understanding of the Bible and the "rules."

Based on my firsthand experience of wildly insane encounters and miraculous healings, there was no question in my mind that God could and would do ANYTHING for His children. Let's be honest here; God could turn planet Earth purple if He wanted to snap His fingers and do so. *Then* what are you going to say about that? Will you challenge God's creative control because He stepped outside your understanding of what has been written?

God could bend our entire reality to His will in less than a split second, and He did that for me on many occasions. You can't say, "Hey God, stop that! What you're doing doesn't line up with scripture!" NO WAY! Dictate to and limit God? I don't think so. Let me rephrase that... You CAN'T do so. Because HE'S GOD!

It was amazing to have had many people from the believer community walk with me post-encounter, but as time went on, I sensed a significant growth spurt that was in store, and it could only occur if my walk with some sadly came to a close. It was time to move forward with God, not look back, and soon enough, He would do something that I never thought would happen in a million years.

Enter...
The Anointed Tow Truck Lady

While driving on the freeway in my Jeep and Mom riding shotgun, we headed into a rough part of town, almost an hour from where we lived. Our family LOVED themselves a good taco, and risking our lives for this one specific mouthwatering taco truck, Azteca, was worth it! Plus, it was almost Christmas, which meant enjoying some holiday treats!

Mom pointed out, "This is the exit your sister usually takes to get the tacos. Let's go this way instead of following the navigation."

After taking the exit, my Jeep unexpectedly stalled. Although we were caught off guard, peace surrounded the incident as I suspiciously commented, "Okay, something's up."

After hanging a quick right at the bottom of the off-ramp, I glided into the only available curbside parking spot—the first one on the right—as my Jeep immediately zonked out!

To our right were worn-down shops, and across the street to our left was the police department. Turning to Mom, I said, "God set us up with some protection in case things get too crazy around here. That's cool!"

We sat silently after calling roadside assistance as this thought crossed my mind: *"Bummer. We drove all this way only to be 1.4 miles away from Azteca Tacos. I wonder if the tow truck guy would be willing to take us there."* Moments later, Mom gently suggested, "We should ask the tow truck guy to take us to Azteca." But would he?

Well, first of all ... "he" wasn't a "he." "He" was a SHE. Our tow truck guy ended up being a tow truck gal! Pulling up past my Jeep, a shiny red tow truck displaying a logo of a sled dog came to a hefty stop. After running up to the passenger's side window and peering in, I was pleasantly surprised to find a petite yet robust Latina woman who not only looked like she could hang with the boys but coincidentally enough, looked Aztec in heritage!

Then, a double take! That brightness—it was all around her—I knew that light!

Instantly inspired, I was encouraged to ask, "Hey, thanks for coming. Look, my mom and I drove almost an hour to get tacos from this taco truck—there's only 1.4 miles left to reach it"—but Tow Truck Lady was way ahead of me! She excitedly interjected, "Oh, you want me to take you there!?" What a shockingly refreshing gesture! I jumped for joy and offered to buy her a burrito—"What kind do you like? Carne asada or chicken?" Tow Truck Lady shrugged it off, deciding, "Um, I don't know, either one is fine—okay, *chieeecken*, I'll take *chieeecken!*"

With my Jeep in tow and to-go bags filled with burritos and tacos, we cruised down the highway in Tow Truck Lady's big red truck, heading toward our town.

We sat side by side, cozied up against each other, as Tow Truck Lady went on about how much she loved her challenging job and even joked about how Mom could do what she does. Mom disagreed, "Oh no, I am getting too old." Tow Truck Lady responded, *"Noooo* you no look old, you like *waah? Fity-faiiive?"* Mom revealed, *"Dis* April, I will be seventy." Tow Truck Lady was shocked—*"Waaaa? Nooo!* You no look *sehveney!"* Mom explained, "If I am fifty-five, *den* it means I have my son when I am ten years old." Tow Truck Lady peered over at me and inquisitively asked, "How old your son??" Mom curiously asked, *"How old you give him?"* Tow Truck Lady gazed at me and guessed, "I *donne* know, *laiike,* twenty-five? Something *laiike daat?"* Bursting into excitement, my response to her was, "Thank you! You saying that made it worth having my Jeep break down today!" She and Mom laughed hysterically for a moment ... then settled into prolonged silence.

The atmosphere inside the vehicle became very still ... a tangible change could be sensed. Tow Truck Lady caught my attention as she investigatively gazed over at me again, but this time with a purpose. Something was different... Her eyes shimmered, indicating authority. Then ... without warning, she proclaimed with full power, "No ... you TWENY-THREE," nodding in certainty and confirming again, *"Yah* ... you TWENY-THREE." Right then, something jolted loose inside me and a seemingly youthful energy took over!

*Months prior, while at the Texas apartments,
I heard God declare, "I am going to give you
your life back." After my fair share of challenges,
why would He want to give all that back to
me? I was happy dedicating myself to Him
while strictly covered under His presence.*

*Give me back my life? No, thank you!
I had the Holy Spirit with me &
that was more than enough!*

Flash forward to Mom and I saying our goodbyes to Tow Truck Lady after being dropped off in front of our house. We sent her on her way with chocolates, a nice little tip, a celebratory "Merry Christmas," and of course, the chicken burrito!

Tow Truck Lady's declaration stuck with me for the rest of the day. *Why did being told I looked twenty-three mean so much?* Appearing "25" was a nice enough compliment, but there had to be something special about "23."

Later on that night, there was a strong pull toward my room; I eventually found myself sitting quietly on my bed, bracing for the unknown when—SUDDENLY—AN EXPLOSIVE FLASH blinded me as it brought about the appearance of a gigantic filmstrip displaying my life's timeline!

It floated right in front of my face and rewound aggressively—*faster and faster and faster*—then, a sudden STOP!

The filmstrip zoomed in to reveal me— at twenty-three, living on my own at the Floribunda Avenue house. I gazed momentarily at this version of me, relishing in his confidence and snarkiness—his witty playfulness and flirtatious charm. This version of *Nick* loved life, and I hadn't seen him in a long time ... I missed this *Nick—a chill ran down my body.*

"Had I always been that way?" The scene immediately zoomed out to reveal the filmstrip—it rapidly rewound to the tail end of me at twenty-two—living with my amazing

family on Sanchez Avenue but bound by their expectations—*that wasn't the real me.*

Almost instantly, the filmstrip quickly zoomed back out of that scene and fast-forwarded to me at twenty-four to reveal—the breakup that would rip me away from my true self, catalyzing years of heartbreaking scenarios that would occur through various means, but play the same story of betrayal and loss on repeat—*that wasn't me either.*

WAIT A SECOND!

I took control of the filmstrip, promptly demanding—*rewind, rewind, rewind*—BOOM! I was dropped right back into the Floribunda house for a second look! And that's when it hit! The only time in my ENTIRE life that I existed as my TRUE SELF was at the age of TWENTY-THREE!

It was Nick outside of family influences, outside of a blindingly toxic relationship, and outside of a post-breakup trauma that would manifest itself in various forms throughout the years!

TWENTY-THREE!

It was one full year of living as the unaffected version of my true self! THAT was the REAL me!

Instantaneously, the floodgates burst open, and what felt like a gigantic tsunami wave baptized my entire body!

God left my year of twenty-three as a bookmark: an insurance policy that would guide me back to who He created me to be! Tow Truck Lady's voice echoed in my soul:

"You TWENTY-THREEE."

As I stared lovingly at my twenty-three-year-old self, I caught his attention. He smiled back at me, transformed into Superman, took flight, and aggressively punched through multiple brick walls until he arrived in the present, hovering right behind me. He confidently wadded his fist and landed one powerful punch right through the center of my back, making us ONE!

A gong was heard...

Blinking a few times, I regained my bearings and looked around my room in awe. For the first time in a very long time, I was seeing it through the eyes of my TRUE SELF!

Bursting into tears, a realization hit... That I had awakened from a 20-year spiritual coma.

Tears and laughter overflowed with my understanding of what had been God's perfect design—losing myself to find Him: only then would I come to know who I truly was.

With this realization, the filmstrip displaying my life's timeline reappeared; it was immediately spliced right before meeting my future ex, including all the mayhem that ensued for years after ... and was re-edited and spliced back together with the present moment!

I was given a do-over! God had released me back into the world after having given me back my life, just like He had promised...

It was a gift that only He could have given: an early Christmas present ... hand-delivered by the most unlikely of all candidates ... a simple lady ... with a red *(sled dog themed)* tow truck.

Rushing out of my bedroom and bursting into the kitchen, I jarred Mom with a sudden entrance. My eyes watered as I stared at her in excitement ... smiled broadly ... and announced ...

"Mom ... I'm back."

"YOU TWENTY-THREE"

PSALM 23:

The LORD is my shepherd; I shall not want. He makes me lie down in green pastures. He leads me beside still waters. He restores my soul. He leads me in paths of righteousness for his name's sake. Even though I walk through the valley of the shadow of death, I will fear no evil, for you are with me: your rod and your staff they comfort me. You prepare a table before me in the presence of my enemies; you anoint my head with oil; my cup overflows. Surely goodness and mercy shall follow me all the days of my life, and I shall dwell in the house of the LORD forever.

I found Him, Grandpa.

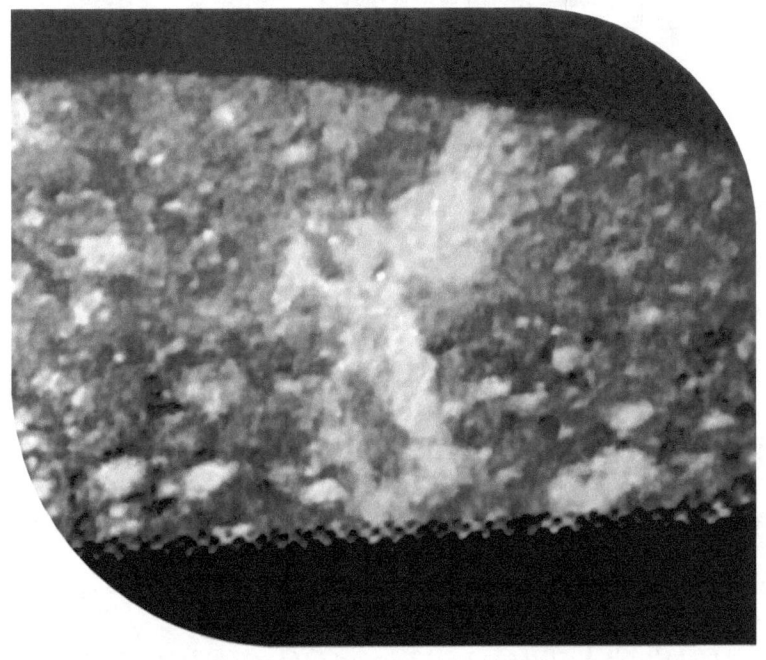

The night before my flight to Atlanta, Georgia
for the Season 3 premiere of The Chosen,
I prayed for Archangel Michael to protect my
flight. After getting into my Jeep to head to the
airport the following morning, this was
frosted on my windshield.

ABOUT THE AUTHOR

NICK SHAKOOUR is best known for his breakout role as Zebedee on the globally acclaimed series *The Chosen.* He has starred in the Oscar-qualifying film *MADARAN (Mothers),* recurred on NBC's *State of Affairs* as Aleek Al Moosari, and voiced Grumpy Bear and Tenderheart Bear for the animated series, *Care Bears: Unlock the Magic.* Nick is the voice of Artichoke and Auntie Uncle on Netflix's Emmy-nominated series *Buddy Thunderstruck* and has voiced a plethora of interactive games, including *Dying Light* as the voice of Savvy and Bilal and *Skylanders* as the voice of Fling Kong.

TRANSFORMER
AWAKENING FROM A
SPIRITUAL COMA

Edited by
Nickolas Shakoour & Caroline Khachoyan

Special Thanks
Petrell Özbay

United States Copyright Office Registration Number:
TXu 2-434-709

Library of Congress Cataloging-in-Publication Data: 2024918642
ISBN: 979-8-9912395-4-7

Stay in touch:
transformer.autobiography@gmail.com

www.ingramcontent.com/pod-product-compliance
Lightning Source LLC
Chambersburg PA
CBHW030909120626
46554CB00001B/70